HARD ROCK FACTS
for a
ROCK HARD FAITH

Life Changing Scientific
and Other Biblical Facts

By

Larry Hoffeditz

Introduction

How can anyone know the Bible is the Word of God, not man? Many may say it's a book with good principles, but also full of fairy tales. A world-wide flood, the Red Sea parting, food falling from heaven, a donkey talking, an axe head floating, the sun standing still, water turned to wine, and a man walking on water. Really?

How can someone believe and have faith in someone they have never seen? Exodus 33:20 says no one may see God and live.

Everyone believes in people and things they have never seen. History books and media are full of them. We often base our beliefs on what someone else has seen. But who has ever seen God?

There's even the argument: Just because the Bible says it's God's Word, doesn't prove it is.

Unfortunately, many Christians have faith in the Bible and the person of the Lord Jesus Christ based on the teachings and experiences of others and their own. They know little, if any, of the scientific, prophetical, and historical facts written in the Bible. Their belief sounds like a "hope" in things unseen. *Now faith is the assurance of things hoped for, the conviction of things not seen* (Hebrews 11:1 ASV). Don't overlook the word "assurance." The King James Version says: *Now faith is the **substance** of things hoped for, the **evidence** of things not seen.* There's abundant substance and evidence for faith in God and the Bible, giving assurance and conviction.

Speaking of Jesus after His resurrection, the Apostle Paul records: *After that, he was seen by more than 500 of his followers at one time, most of whom are still alive, though some have died.* (1 Corinthians 15:6)

God's words were given the writers by God's Holy Spirit. *All Scripture is inspired by God and is useful to teach us what is true and to make us realize what is wrong in our lives. It corrects us when we are wrong and teaches us to do what is right.* (2 Timothy 3:16).

My love of science and the Bible is why you'll find more scientific than historical or prophetical facts in this book. These were recorded in the Bible centuries before modern science discovered them or they were fulfilled. The writers could not have known these facts without supernatural revelation from God. They prove the Bible to be the Word of the only true God.

You will discover a wealth of unique and interesting facts. Read on.

Chapter 1: God's Word or Man's?

How do we know the Bible is God's Word, not man's? The Bible repeatedly says it is God's Word:
- *All Scripture is God-breathed [given by divine inspiration]* (2 Timothy 3:16a AMP).
- *Above all, you must realize that no prophecy in Scripture ever came from the prophet's own understanding, or from human initiative. No, those prophets were moved by the Holy Spirit, and they spoke from God* (2 Peter 1:20).

Someone might protest: "Just because the Bible says it is solely the Word of God does not prove it is."

Often Christians are accused of being like the proverbial ostrich, their head buried in a sand of faith without factual evidence. An abundance of facts exists proving the Bible to be God's Word, not man's. Few people know them.

Scientific, Prophetical and Historical Facts

An indisputable proof is the Bible's scientific, historical, and prophetical facts. It was impossible for the writers of the Bible to know these facts when they wrote them.

A few of the many scientific facts include:

1. Life is in the blood - Leviticus 17:11 (Chapter 4)
2. Stars make sounds - Job 38:7 (Chapter 2)
3. The stars are innumerable - Jeremiah 33:22 (Chapter 2)
4. Human and animal flesh are not the same - 1 Corinthians 15:39 (Chapter 6)
5. The earth is not supported by anything - Job 26:7 (Chapter 9)
6. The earth is round - Isaiah 40:22 (Chapter 10)
7. There are currents in the ocean - Psalm 8:8 (Chapter 5)
8. The hydrological cycle - Job 38:26-27, 26:8; Amos 9:6; Ecclesiastes 1:7 (Chapter 8)

9. There are springs under the sea - Job 38:16 (Chapter 22)
10. The best time for circumcision is on the eighth day - Genesis 17:12 (Chapter 7)

These are known scientific facts today, but not when they were written hundreds or thousands of years ago.

Some were in blatant opposition to current beliefs, especially in the scientific community. For example:

1. For centuries bloodletting was a common practice.
2. Scientists have given an approximate number of stars throughout history.
3. The "common cell theory" was believed by evolutionists for centuries.
4. Years ago, without a witness, hit-and-run drivers when apprehended could claim they hit an animal and they would go free.
5. Many theories in the past record different earth support systems.
6. A flat earth society still exists.
7. Today, circumcision is done soon after birth or even years later.

For more interesting details on these scientific facts read their chapters.

Over three hundred prophecies tell the ancestry, birth, life, ministry, death, resurrection, and ascension of Jesus of Nazareth. All have been fulfilled. They include:

1. Genesis 3:15 - Satan would bruise Jesus' heel, Jesus would crush Satan's head.
2. Isaiah 7:14 - Messiah, Jesus, would be born of a virgin.
3. Isaiah 9:6 - Jesus, would be God in human flesh.
4. Micah 5:2 - Jesus, would be born in Bethlehem Ephratah.
5. Psalm 34:20 - The Roman practice of breaking leg bones of crucified victims would not happen to Jesus.
6. Psalm 16:8-11 - Messiah, Jesus, would be resurrected.

These are a few of the many Messianic prophecies fulfilled by Jesus.

Only one person, Jesus of Nazareth, fulfilled all the messianic prophecies in the Old Testament. He performed countless miracles, taught the most profound words ever uttered, died for the sins of all people, and arose from the dead. Who else has ever done those things?

Over 25 percent of the Bible contains specific fulfilled prophecies. This is true of no other book in the world. A sign of its divine origin. [1]

Read chapters 2-14 for more detailed scientific facts; 15-20 for specific prophetical facts; and 21-24 for comprehensive historical facts.

---

[1] https://jewsforjesus.org/answers/top-40-most-helpful-messianic-prophecies/

Disciples martyred

All of Jesus' twelve disciples, except Judas Iscariot and John died martyr's deaths. They died proclaiming Jesus as Lord and Savior and His message of being the only way to eternal life. Jesus said:

- *I am the way, the truth, and the life. No one can come to the Father except through me.* (John 14:6)
- *Have I been with you all this time, Philip, and yet you still don't know who I am? Anyone who has seen me has seen the Father! So why are you asking me to show him to you?* (John 14:9)
- *The Father and I are one.* (John 10:30)

Why would they die martyr's deaths for a person and message they knew wasn't true? Read chapter 24, "To Die For," for more details.

Other Facts

Other facts proving the Bible to be the unerring Word of God:

1. Thirty-five to forty writers wrote the sixty-six books in the Bible over a period of one thousand five hundred years. Their writings span some three thousand years of history. **All wrote a message of redemption and salvation**:

2. **A unified theme runs throughout the entire Bible**:

   a. **All humans are sinful** - *All of us, like sheep, have strayed away. We have* left God's paths to follow our own. (Isaiah 53:6a) *For everyone has sinned; we all fall short of God's glorious standard.* (Romans 3:23)

   b. **God hates and punishes sin** - *For the wages of sin is death.* (Romans 6:23a) *I, the LORD, will punish the world for its evil and the wicked for their sin.* (Isaiah 13:11a).

   c. **God loves all sinners** - *For this is how God loved the world: He gave his one and only Son, so that everyone who believes in Him will not perish but have eternal life.* (John 3:16)

   d. **Jesus paid for the sin of every human being** - *He himself is the sacrifice that atones for our sins, and not only our sins but the sins of all the world.* (1 John 2:2) *... Yet the LORD laid on him the sins of us all.* (Isaiah 53:6b)

   e. **God freely and completely gives eternal life to anyone and everyone who accepts His free gift of eternal life and trusts Him alone** and nothing or no one else as their only means of eternal life in heaven...*but the free gift of God is eternal life through Christ Jesus our Lord.* (Romans 6:23b) *God saved you by his grace when you believed. And you can't take credit for this; it is a gift from God. Salvation is not a reward for the good things we have done, so none of us can boast about it.* (Ephesians 2:8-9) *Most assuredly, I say to you, he who believes in*

Me has everlasting life. (John 6:47 NKJV) *He saved us, not because of the righteous things we had done, but because of his mercy…"* (Titus 3:5a)

3. **The wide variety of backgrounds and intellects of its writers**. They were real people: shepherds, soldiers, fishermen, a tentmaker. Some were elite: Solomon & David were kings. Others were outcasts: Jeremiah and Joseph were imprisoned, and Elijah was the hunted, as was King David. They lived in a world different from ours. Each answered their calling to communicate what was true, important, and worth recording for future generations.

4. **Man would have not written the Bible the way it is written**, unless writing a fiction book. No way they would have included:
   a. two bears eating children for calling Elisha a "baldhead"- 2 Kings 2:23-25
   b. a donkey talking to Balaam - Numbers 22:21-39
   c. an axe head floating - 2 Kings 6:1-7
   d. manna & quail raining from heaven - Exodus 16-18
   e. the sun standing still - Joshua 10:1-15
   f. God killing thousands of Israelites - Numbers 16 (14,700+); Numbers 25 (24,000); Achan and his entire family for the sin he committed – Joshua 7
   g. David's sin with Bathsheba, premeditated murder of Uriah, and his baby son dying - 2 Samuel 11-12
   h. A total of 160 separate killing sprees and 2,821,364 deaths either directly orchestrated by God or carried out with His assistance or approval. Satan notches up only 10 kills."[2]

These events defy laws of nature or don't fit the character of a loving God. The central theme throughout the Bible is one of redemption and salvation. But God's Word also repeatedly gives accounts of His justice, hatred, and punishment of sin.

Experiential Evidence

Christians all over the world give testimony to the accuracy of God's Word through the repeated fulfillment of His promises, day after day.

Countless experiences validate the words and examples in the Bible. Many times, they are beyond human comprehension or explanation. Everyday experiences exemplify God's presence and work in the lives of born-again believers. My experiences attest to God and His Word being active daily in my life.

God in His endless love for all His creation, especially mankind, had His Word written for everyone to see His love and care for them. He provides a free gift of eternal life in heaven, to anyone and everyone who accepts His payment for all their sin as their only means of salvation.

For this is how God loved the world: He gave his one and only Son, so that everyone who believes in him will not perish but have eternal life. (John 3:16)

---

[2] htpp://www.vocativ.com/news/309748/all-the-people-god-kills-in-the-bible/index.html

Scientific Facts

Chapter 2: Celestial Orchestra

Celestial Orchestra

Stars sing to us. Imagine floating in outer space, listening to a "starry orchestra".

Remember the *Twinkle, Twinkle Little Star* lyrics? Small dots blanket our black night sky, winking at us.

Stars look tiny because they are so far away. But they are enormous. The sun, our closest star, is about 93 million miles away. One million times larger than our earth, its diameter is close to 900,000 miles. One-hundred and nine earths could line up across its face. Yet sometimes it looks as small as a ping-pong ball. Although humongous compared to the earth, it's classified as a G2 yellow dwarf star.

How about Proxima Centauri, our nearest star after the sun? A pee-wee spot in the Centaurus Constellation. It has a distance of 270,000 times farther from us than the sun. Stick those numbers in your calculator: 270,000 times 93,000,000.

Starry Facts
Travel time from earth to the sun:

- 177 years by car @ 60mph
- 21 years by plane @ 500mph
- **Travel time to Proxima Centauri from earth**:
- 19,000 years @ 150,000mph
- in Helios 2, one of our fastest
- spacecrafts.[1]

So Near

It's impossible to imagine the distance stars are from us. Ninety-three million miles to our closest star. Over twenty-five trillion miles to the next closest star. [3]

Our heavenly Father is near to us. He will never leave us. *So be strong and courageous! Do not be afraid and do not panic before them. For the LORD your God will personally go ahead of you. He will neither fail you nor abandon you.* (Deuteronomy 31:6)

A red dwarf star is one of the tiniest types of stars. They're about 1,300 times bigger than our planet. Some kind of "giant dwarfs." Try to imagine 1,300 earths.[4]

By now you're thinking, "brain freeze. Please, no more monstrous numbers."

Here's more shimmering star facts:

- Many stars are bigger and brighter than our sun. There are more stars in the universe than grains of sand on Earth. Try counting a handful of sand.
- Red to blue colored super-giants, have radii about 1,000 times larger than our sun.
- The most massive stars can be two billion miles across.
- The apparent twinkling of stars is caused by movement of the earth's atmosphere.
- Stars are gigantic and innumerable.

> **Galaxy Facts**
>
> **Our Milky Way galaxy**:
>
> - Approximately 250 – 300 billion stars.
>
> - Nearest galaxy is 2 million light years away (1 light year = the distance light travels in 1 year = 6 trillion miles).
>
> - Astronomers estimate there are 100 billion galaxies.

Star Sounds

Scientists now know stars make sounds. These sounds vary in pitch and tone. Astronomer David Kurtz tells us, "*Astronomers found out in the 1970s, the sun and other stars do actually sing.*" Like musical instruments, they produce notes by vibrations. We cannot hear their sounds directly. Astronomers can detect them by looking into the cores of stars. Ghostly whistling, drumming, humming, or rumbling sounds emerge from these glowing spheres.

How do you get singing out of those sounds? Pallab Ghosh, a Science correspondent for BBC News in an article titled, "Music from the Stars", states, "The sound of one star is slightly different from others. This is because the sound they make depends on their age, size and chemical composition."[5] Can you imagine an orchestra with zillions of instruments each making a different sound a little higher or lower than the others? What a creator our God is!

---

[3] http://www.universetoday.com/15403/how-long-would-it-take-to-travel-to-the-nearest-star

[4] http://www.universetoday.com/24670/red-dwarf-stars/

Sing On

Like the stars, God wants us to sing to Him. *Come, let us sing to the LORD! Let us shout joyfully to the Rock of our salvation* (Psalm 95:1). How good we sound is not important. Our praise is to Him. We're told to make a "joyful noise." Everyone can make noise. Singing noise is joyful to the Lord.

Bible Star Facts

These are amazing facts, but not surprising if we carefully read the Bible. Job, the oldest book in the Bible, written some 3,500 years ago, declares, *As the morning stars sang together, and all the angels shouted for joy?* (Job 38:7) There is no way Job could have known stars sing without God telling him.

How about these star facts? God knows how many stars there are and gives each one a name. *He counts the stars and calls them all by name.* (Psalm 147:4) Wait a minute, a name for each star? How can God do that? Our galaxy has over 200 billion stars. There are an estimated 100 billion other galaxies. Counting them is mind boggling.

Shine On

Just like the stars, God wants us to shine for Him. *In the same way, let your good deeds shine out for all to see, so that everyone will praise your heavenly Father* (Matthew 5:16).

Sing the stanzas from *Twinkle, Twinkle, Little Star,* written by Jane Taylor (1783–1824):

> Twinkle, twinkle, little star, How I wonder what you are.
> Up above the world so high, Like a diamond in the sky.
>
> When the blazing sun is gone, When he nothing shines upon,
> Then you show your little light, Twinkle, twinkle, all the night.
>
> Then the traveler in the dark, Thanks you for your tiny spark,
> He could not see which way to go, if you did not twinkle so.
>
> In the dark blue sky you keep, and often through my curtains peep,
> For you never shut your eye, till the sun is in the sky.
> As your bright and tiny spark, lights the traveler in the dark.
> Though I know not what you are, twinkle, twinkle, little star.
>
> Twinkle, twinkle, little star. how I wonder what you are.
> Up above the world so high, like a diamond in the sky.

It's great to have factual, scientific evidence for God, His creation, and His Word, the Bible. Remember these facts when gazing into a starry sky.

Someday, I'll listen to God's celestial orchestra. Will you?

Chapter 3: The Biggest Bang Ever

My arm stretched upward. One squishy red gummy bear in hand. I asked my chemistry class, "How many of you have eaten a gummy bear?" All hands shot up. "What about a whole hand full?" Most students raised their hands. "How about the entire bag?" A lot responded with a giggle. "I'm going to show you how much energy is in one little gummy bear."

Safety goggles on, the propane torch was lit. In seconds the potassium chlorate catalyst (a catalyst starts or speeds up a chemical reaction) in the bottom of the test tube liquefied. Dropping the gummy bear from tongs into the test tube, I jumped back. In an instant, an explosion of intense heat, light, and smoke erupted. I warned students not to touch the test tube to avoid a third-degree burn. A burnt marshmallow smell wafted through the room.

Warning: Please don't try this dangerous experiment without caution, safety goggles, protective apron, and no one close to where it's being done.

Atoms were not split in this experiment. By rearranging them we saw the tremendous escaping energy.

Atoms make up everything in our entire universe. One or more atoms of the 118 known chemical elements compose any existing substance.

Positively charged protons and "no charge" neutrons reside in the central nucleus. Negatively charged electrons buzz around the core.

Opposite charges attract. Like charges repel each other. Protons are packed in an atom's nucleus and electrons circle them. Hold on. Tightly bunched positives, explosion time. How could they be held together?

Super-Duper Glue

What holds an infinite number of atoms in a vast universe together? We're talking millions of galaxies, zillions of stars, oceans with a gargantuan amount of water, and innumerable people, plants, and animals. Googols (1 googol = 10^{100}) of atoms roaming all over the place.

Some scientists propose "atomic glue", a "non-electric residual strong force," or "gluons and quarks" holding atoms together. A kind of super-duper glue? Unseen and un-isolated forces.

Origin of atoms

Maybe if we knew how atoms were made, we might understand what keeps them from exploding. If you don't believe in God, a primeval soup with the right mixture of chemicals and a spark might be given. A Big Bang collision of celestial bodies could be proposed.

A major scientific hurdle for these biogenesis theories is the universally accepted First Law of Thermodynamics. It states matter cannot be created or destroyed. Where did the first stuff come from? No matter what you start with, something had to bring it into existence. More faith is required to believe everything evolved from some initial substance, than to accept a supernatural creator.

Attraction

I have two huge magnets, each being the size of a large hand. They have tremendous power. When like poles get close, a strong force pushes them apart. Align opposite poles and they smash together. Don't get your fingers in between them.

Some of my students, especially the big tough guys, would try to push like poles together while keeping their arms straight. Did anyone ever do it? Not!

Explosion

What happens when an atom explodes? Atomic bombs dropped on Hiroshima and Nagasaki showed the mega result of atomic explosion. Tremendous white hot heat melts or vaporizes everything in its path. Temperatures reach 100,000,000 °C. Blinding, intense light radiates for miles and miles. A roaring blast accompanies the explosion.

Wonderfully Made

The average human contains 7×10^{27} atoms. A seven with twenty-seven zeroes behind it, or twenty-seven billion, billion, billions. What an amazing and awesome God and Savior we have. *Thank you for making me so wonderfully complex! Your workmanship is marvelous - how well I know it* (Psalm 139:14).

Power Packed Words

The first verse in Genesis states, *"In the beginning God created the heavens and the earth."* A similar phrase is repeated in each of the six days of creation in which every basic life form was

Nuclear Explosion

Nuclear power plants produce huge amounts of energy generated by splitting small amounts of Uranium atoms.

Nuclear fuel contains at least ten million times more energy than a chemical fuel like gasoline.

The Chernobyl nuclear plant disaster showed the far-reaching effects and tremendous energy released by splitting atoms. A radioactive cloud spread over most of Europe from this serious nuclear accident.

made. *"Then God **said**, let there be…"* in Genesis 1:3, 6, 9, 11, 14, 20, 24, 26, and 29. God did not pour some chemicals into a test tube, stir them around, and presto a bird, fish, tree, horse, and human popped out. He spoke and life came into existence.

The New Testament reinforces the creation account in the first chapter of John, verses 1-6. It speaks of Jesus, the Word, being God the creator: *In the beginning the Word already existed. The Word was with God, and the Word was God. He existed in the beginning with God. God created everything through Him, and nothing was created except through Him. The Word gave life to everything that was created, and his life brought light to everyone. The light shines in the darkness, and the darkness can never extinguish it.*

Believing all life forms came from one primeval cell or a Big Bang takes a lot of blind faith. Chapter 12, entitled *Missing Links* and chapter 13, *Other Evolutionary Problems,* presents a lot more hurdles in the way of evolutionary theories.

Bible Fact

Second Peter 3:7, 9-12, written almost 2,000 years ago, gives an accurate account of an atomic explosion. There is no way Peter could have known what an atom or an element was, or what happens when they explode. Listen to God's descriptive words in this amazing account:

And by the same word, the present heavens and earth have been stored up for fire. They are being kept for the day of judgment, when ungodly people will be destroyed.

*But the day of the Lord will come as unexpectedly as a thief. **Then the heavens will pass away with a terrible noise, and the very elements themselves will disappear in fire**, and the earth and everything on it will be found to deserve judgment. Since **everything around us is going to be destroyed like this**, what holy and godly lives you should live, looking forward to the day of God and hurrying it along. On that day, **he will set the heavens on fire, and the elements will melt away in the flames.***

Imagine the result from every atom in our universes exploding. Whoa! We've never seen those kinds of fireworks! Not a Big Bang, the BIGGEST bang ever.

No Fear

Do we need to fear a nuclear war or God saying, "That's All Folks!" like Porky Pig said at the end of his Looney Tunes cartoons? The same God who created everything by His spoken word and holds all things together, *...he holds all creation together* (Colossians 1:17*),* could in a like manner end it with a few words.

Jesus will return to take all His children home to heaven. The passage in 2 Peter 3:13 ends with these words: *But we are looking forward to the new heavens and new earth He has promised, a world filled with God's righteousness.*

As born-again believers, with our trust in the complete payment the Lord Jesus Christ has made for all sin (1 John 2:2), we have this promise from God's Word, the Bible: ... *looking forward to the coming of God's Son from heaven—Jesus, whom God raised from the dead. He is the one who has rescued us from the terrors of the coming judgment.* (1 Thessalonians 1:10).

Christians need not fear the BIGGEST bang ever!

Chapter 4: Bloody Red and White Stripes

If you lived in ancient Egypt or Greece and had an infection, a "doctor" would probably take blood out of you using a metal lancet, a sharpened piece of wood, or leeches. You might be given medications if the disease kept hanging on. But often you were bled again and again. This common practice was called bloodletting.

Letting blood out of a person regularly was believed to keep them healthy. Bloodletting the sick was thought to rid them of disease.

Our red and white stripped barber pole originated from a bloody white rag, towel or bandage being hung outside the shops of blood-letters. Their common practice was to let blood out of customers. Haircuts were a side option.[5]

One possible cause of, or contribution to, George Washington's death was bloodletting. His doctors, including Dr. Benjamin Rush, were strong advocates of bloodletting. They weren't quacks. Dr. Benjamin Rush signed the Declaration of Independence, had the title "The Father of American Medicine," and wrote the first American chemistry textbook.

President Washington loved to ride horses. On Thursday, December 12, 1799, he rode for five hours inspecting his Mount Vernon estate. The weather was snowy, mixed with hail, freezing rain and a cold wind. He stopped to help free a carriage stuck in the snow. Without changing his wet clothes, he arrived home and ate supper. The next morning, he complained of a severe sore throat. He became hoarse and soon could not swallow.[6]

---

[5] http://en.wikipedia.org/wiki/Barber's_pole
[6] http://en.wikipedia.org/wiki/George_Washington

His wife, Martha, immediately called their estate overseer, Colonel Tobias Lear. She sent couriers to his doctors. At Mr. Washington's request, Colonel Lear bled him. His doctors repeatedly removed his blood. Half or more of his blood was removed in less than sixteen hours. It is still debated whether his primary cause of death was bloodletting or a throat infection. Bloodletting accelerated his death, even if it did not cause it. It's amazing the practice of bloodletting was still an accepted and trusted practice by some in America.[1]

For centuries, physicians believed illnesses resulted from having too much blood. Many believed by letting out blood, they were letting out disease. It was a common practice to regularly have some blood removed in order to stay healthy. Some primitive peoples still believe this process lets out evil spirits.[7]

Life

The Bible said over 3,000 years ago, *for the life of the body is in its blood.* Leviticus 17:11a.

Today we know blood carries disease. But you do not get rid of disease by letting out large amounts of blood. Nor is weekly blood-letting a means of staying healthy. Blood is essential for life. The Bible said it long before bloodletting originated and before we scientifically knew the bloody facts.

Atonement

Leviticus 17:11 is also a prophecy of the coming Messiah Jesus, *for the life of the body is in its blood. I have given you the blood on the altar to purify you, making you right with the LORD. It is the blood, given in exchange for a life, that makes purification possible.*

The Lord Jesus Christ is our atonement. What is atonement? It is the way God paid for all the things you or I ever have or ever will do wrong, our sins. In Old Testament times, a sacrifice of the best animal available was offered up to ask God for His forgiveness. This could not remove their sin. Only the ultimate sacrifice made by Jesus could atone or pay for all sin. The perfect God-man, Jesus, gave his life—his blood—as the only possible means of atonement for the past, present, and future sins of everyone. Hebrews 10:1-4 makes it crystal clear: *The old system under the law of Moses was only a shadow, a dim preview of the good things to come, not the good things themselves. The sacrifices under that system were repeated again and again, year after year, but they were never able to provide perfect cleansing for those who came to worship. If they could have provided perfect cleansing, the sacrifices would have stopped, for the worshipers would have been purified once for all time, and their feelings of guilt would have disappeared. But instead, those sacrifices actually reminded them of their sins year after year. For it is not possible for the blood of bulls and goats to take away sins.*

Instead, *He himself is the sacrifice that atones for our sins—and not only our sins but the sins of all the world* (1 John 2:2). Every person who accepts His atoning payment for all their sins is assured of and freely given eternal life.

---

[7] http://en.wikipedia.org/wiki/Bloodletting

Life is in blood. Eternal life is through the shed blood of Jesus. Accept His complete payment for all your sin and He gives you the best life, everlasting life.

Christ's bloody red stripes paid for all our sins. They provide His perfect righteousness needed making us as white as snow (Isaiah 1:18). Don't bury your head in the sand of unbelief.

CAUTION: Blood carries disease. Never play around with it or come in contact with someone else's blood.

Chapter 5: Paths in the Sea

Fish go to schools. They quickly learn a school is the best place to be. A cool place to have fun with friends. Food is usually good, except when a big bully swipes yours. Most importantly, schools can provide protection and less effort on ocean voyages.

The bottom line is fish live in a fascinating world.

Ever heard of a Christmas Tree Worm? How about a Sea Cucumber? A Blobfish? Oooh, a Viperfish or a Longhorn Cowfish? Try looking at their pictures without laughing. Thousands of weird names and interesting ocean creatures. Shows God's sense of humor when creating them. I'll bet He laughed out loud.

Blob Fish

There are over five-hundred different species of sharks.[8] Are they our friends or enemies? The mention of their name brings fear to many. Especially after watching "Jaws."

We know little about the home of zillions of watery creatures?

- About 50 to 80% of all life on earth is in the ocean.
- Oceans cover 71% of the earth's surface.
- Less than 10% of the oceans have been explored by humans.
- The average depth of the ocean is more than forty-one football fields, 3,795 meters.

---

[8] https://ocean.si.edu/ocean-life/sharks-rays

- Scientists have named and classified around 1.5 million species of marine life. How many names can you think of?
- An estimated 50 million more species are undiscovered.
- The oceans contain 97% of our water. Less than 1% is fresh.
- 90% of all volcanic activity occurs in our oceans. "Lob", "lots of bubbles".
- The top ten feet of the ocean holds as much heat as our entire atmosphere. Doesn't feel warm during winter.
- Each year three times more garbage is dumped in oceans than the weight of fish caught. We need "garbage preventers" more than "garbage collectors".
- The greatest percentage of the world's protein eaten by humans comes from fish.
- More than 90% of the trade between countries is carried by ships.
- About half of the communications between nations use underwater cables. Ever try to speak underwater? Here comes more bubbles.[9]

Is the ocean important to us? Duh! Ninety-seven percent of the earth is water; 50 - 80% of all life lives in it; and 90% of world trade uses it. It's our greatest source of protein and generates more heat than our atmosphere. It's not just important, it's vital to life.

Matthew Maury is noted as the "Father of Oceanography." He was in the U.S. Navy for most of his life. An astronomer, historian, oceanographer, meteorologist, cartographer (map/chart maker), author, geologist, and educator make for an impressive resume. He charted the winds and currents of the ocean.

How did he know there were currents and wind patterns in the ocean?

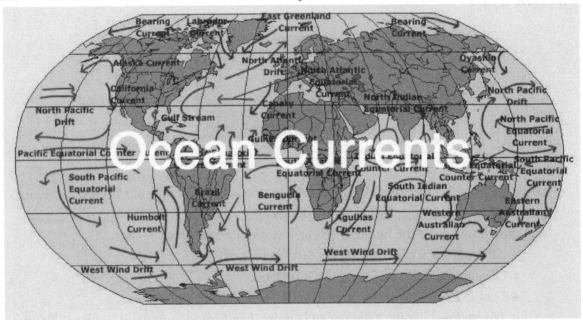

---

[9] http://marinebio.org/marinebio/facts/index.asp

In *A Life of Matthew Fontaine Maury* his daughter states, "Matthew's father was very exact in the religious training of his family." She tells how he would gather all nine children both morning and night to read the Psalms. Matthew became intimately familiar with the Bible. He could quote much of it and give chapter and verse. After his death, His Bible is depicted on a monument dedicated to him.[10]

Maury devoted himself to studying the winds, clouds, weather, and ocean features, as well as the Bible. One day when he was ill, his oldest son was reading Psalm 8 to him. Matthew asked him to repeat Psalm 8:8. The words of this verse stuck in his mind: *The birds of the air, And the fish of the sea that pass through the paths of the seas* (NKJV).

Matthew thought, "If God's Word said there were 'paths' in the seas, then there must be paths." He set out to find them.[11][12] Find them he did and charted them. In 1855 Matthew Maury wrote the first extensive and comprehensive book on oceanography, *The Physical Geography of the Sea*. He charted winds and ocean currents, including ocean lanes for ships at sea. He included Biblical passages of meteorological and other scientific importance.

He charted winds and ocean currents, including ocean lanes for ships at sea. His navigational charts transformed the sailing industry. Some shipping lane times were reduced by more than one-half. The monetary benefit was and remains phenomenal.[13]

A monument erected by the state of Virginia in his memory reads: "Matthew Fontaine Maury, Pathfinder of the Seas, the genius who first snatched from the oceans and atmosphere the secret of their laws. His inspiration, Holy Writ, Psalm 8:8; Ecclesiastes 1:6." A genius? No, just a simple Bible-believing Christian who trusted the inerrancy of the Word of God.

How did the psalmist know there were "Paths in the sea?" Psalm 8:8 was written at least 1800 years before Matthew Maury. Simple, God told the writer of Psalm 8 and his writing told Mr. Maury.

The Bible's scientific facts keep coming. No sticking heads in the sand?

---

[10] http://en.wikipedia.org/wiki/Matthew_Fontaine_Maury

[11] "Paths of The Sea"; Duane Gish, Ph.D.

[12] http://www.answersingenesis.org/articles/cm/v11/n3/maury

[13] https://transportgeography.org/contents/chapter1/emergence-of-mechanized-transportation-systems/maury-navigation-sailing-1850/

Chapter 6: Hit and Run Drivers

For centuries many scientists subscribed to the "common cell theory." They believed the cells of all living organisms were identical. Makes sense if you believe in evolution. If everything came from one cell, then all cells of every living organism should be the same or similar.

In 1590, along came the microscope (Zaccharias). We discovered that all cells were not the same. Animal cells were quite different from plant cells. Both were different from human cells.

Even with all this knowledge there was a problem. A hit-and-run driver could say they hit an animal. Unless there was a witness, they could go free.

While attending college, a professor told our class of a recent scientific discovery. He said a lab test was now able to distinguish between animal and human flesh samples. Parke-Davis, a major pharmaceutical company, had developed an anti-human precipitin test.

Was I interested? I was in my fourth year at St. Louis College of Pharmacy before getting drafted into the Army. I had worked in pharmacies for six years and was currently working in one while attending college.

I wrote Parke-Davis asking for information about their test. Their reply shocked me. They did not know of a similar test, let alone have one. The professor couldn't find the article he had read.

This shows the importance of verifying what anyone tells you, no matter who it is. When it comes to information about the Bible, this is especially true. Base your beliefs on God's Word, not man's.

Unfortunately, I had been using this information about the Parke Davis test on a survey asking college students if they knew different scientific facts in the Bible. Oops!

Not willing to give up, I contacted Miami University's forensic department. When told what the test was for, they told me they used such a test. Dr. Weiner developed it. Given his contact information, I verified the origin of this test. Now they could tell the difference between an animal and a human sample taken in a hit and run investigation.

Another source gives discovery credit to Paul Theodor Uhlenhuth, a German bacteriologist and immunologist. He was a Professor at the University of Strasbourg and is famous in the annals of forensic science or developing the species precipitin test. Known as the Uhlenhuth test, it could distinguish human blood from animal blood. It was developed in 1901, a discovery which had tremendous importance in criminal justice in the 20th century.[14]

Biblical Fact

Written around 55AD, 1 Corinthians 15:39 states, *Similarly there are different kinds of flesh - one kind for humans, another for animals, another for birds, and another for fish.*

Over 1900 years ago, long before there were microscopes, or before we could prove this well-known fact, God revealed it to Paul. He wrote it in the Bible.

Can you imagine Paul asking, "How does God know all this stuff?" Not! Paul knew God created all life. He writes in Romans 1:20, *For ever since the world was created, people have seen the earth and sky. Through everything God made, they can clearly see his invisible qualities: his eternal power and divine nature. So, they have no excuse for not knowing God.*

Whose head is in sand?

---

[14] https://www.americanforensics.org/uhlenhuth-test/

Chapter 7: Why Day Eight Circumcision?

Why were Jewish babies circumcised on the eighth day of their life in Bible times? Parents did it because God commanded them to. *From generation to generation, every male child must be circumcised on the eighth day after his birth. This applies not only to members of your family but also to the servants born in your household and the foreign-born servants whom you have purchased* (Genesis 17:12).

Today, most U.S. males are circumcised within two days of birth, states WebMD. Pain is minimal and not remembered if done early. Bleeding and infection are rare problems and can be easily treated by doctors with clotting procedures or medicine. Circumcision can also be performed later in a child or adult's life.

More pain and risk are involved the older a male is. I was in my fifties when I was circumcised without any complications, except the pain. Ouch!

Still the questions, why did God command a specific day for circumcision? Why wait eight days? Get it over with.

One problem with circumcision is bleeding. Today, bleeding is usually slight and can be controlled by direct pressure, application of gauze or a gel, or other procedures.

None of these, except direct pressure, were available in Bible times. One might think, wouldn't sooner be better.

Again, the question, Why the eighth day?

Only God knew the medical fact we now know. No surprise, He created the human body, prothrombin, and vitamin K. What did no one else know, except God?

On the eighth day of a male human's life, they have the highest concentration of prothrombin they will ever have in their lifetime. What is prothrombin? It is a plasma protein involved in blood coagulation. Prothrombin is formed by and stored in the liver.

Bert Thompson, PhD, in his article entitled *Biblical Accuracy and Circumcision on the 8th Day* states, "In 1935, professor H. Dam proposed the name 'vitamin K' for the factor in foods that helped prevent hemorrhaging in baby chicks. We now know vitamin K is responsible for the production (by the liver) of the element known as prothrombin. If vitamin K is deficient, there will be a prothrombin deficiency and hemorrhaging may occur. Oddly, it is only on the fifth through the seventh days of the newborn male's life that vitamin K (produced by bacteria in the intestinal tract) is present in adequate quantities. Vitamin K, coupled with prothrombin, causes blood coagulation, which is important in any surgical procedure."

Holt and McIntosh, in their classic work, *Holt Pediatrics*, observed that a newborn infant has "peculiar susceptibility to bleeding between the second and fifth days of life. Hemorrhages at this time, though often inconsequential, are sometimes extensive; they may produce serious damage to internal organs, especially to the brain, and cause death from shock and exsanguination" (1953, pp. 125-126). Since vitamin K is not produced in sufficient quantities until days five through seven, it would be wise to postpone any surgery until sometime after day five. But why did God specify day eight?

On the eighth day, the amount of prothrombin present is elevated above 100% of normal and is the only day in the male's life in which this will be the case under normal conditions. If surgery is to be performed, day eight is the perfect day to do it. Vitamin K and prothrombin levels are at their peak. A chart published by McMillen and Stern in their book, *None of These Diseases*, portrays this in graphic form.

Wow! The safest day in an infant's life for circumcision is day eight, even if you have other ways to control bleeding. Allowing God's natural creation to do its job would even be more desirable and less painful than applying pressure. Oh, yeah!

God knows what's best for us from birth to the grave. *For I know the plans I have for you, says the LORD. They are plans for good and not for disaster, to give you a future and a hope.* (Jeremiah 29:11)

Listen to how well God knows His creation even before conception: *You made all the delicate, inner parts of my body and knit me together in my mother's womb. Thank you for making me so wonderfully complex! Your workmanship is marvelous—how well I know it. You watched me as I was being formed in utter seclusion, as I was woven together in the dark of the womb. You saw me before I was born. Every day of my life was recorded in your book. Every moment was laid out before a single day had passed. How precious are your thoughts about me, O God. They cannot be numbered! I can't even count them; they outnumber the grains of sand! And when I wake up, you are still with me!* (Psalm 139:13-18)

The Bible is full of hard-rock facts for a rock-hard faith.

Chapter 8: Round and Round Hydrological Cycle

It never ends. Once a merry-go-round, starts it keeps going round and round. Never stopping until whatever was pushing it ran out of energy.

From the beginning of time, a cycle has never stopped. There have been pauses, even for a long time, but it doesn't go away. What is it? The water cycle, or scientifically, the hydrological cycle. A process essential to all life.

This cycle is the three-step process of evaporation, condensation, and precipitation. It keeps going on and on, round and round. We know this process, but some were probably scratching their heads over how this kept happening a few thousand years ago.

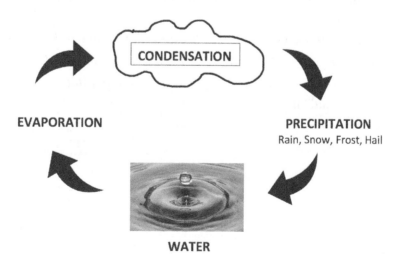

Listen to a description Job gave over two thousand years ago: *He draws up* (KJV *"maketh small"*) *the water vapor* (evaporation) *and then distills* (condensation) *it into rain. The rain pours down* (precipitation) *from the clouds, and everyone benefits* (Job 36:27-28). Job could not know this process without God's inspiration. No way!

This continual water cycle is vital to all life on the earth. How much of the earth is water? Almost three-fourths. The human body is approximately two-thirds water. All living things need water to grow and survive. No wonder God created a natural cyclical process to keep everything alive.

Water evaporates, condenses into clouds, which eventually pours down precipitation in the form of rain, snow, sleet, or hail. Even dew condenses from cooled water vapor above the ground.

Job 26:8 presents an interesting query: *He wraps the rain in his thick clouds, and the* clouds don't burst with the weight. The AMS adds: *which otherwise would spill on earth all at once.* What a mess. But it doesn't happen. Amazing!

Job extols God in Job 28:26-27, "*He made the laws for the rain and laid out a path for the lightning. Then he saw wisdom and evaluated it. He set it in place and examined it thoroughly.*"

After all that Job suffered:
- death of ten children,
- loss of more than eleven thousand livestock and many servants,
- excruciating pus-filled sores all over his body,
- his wife telling him to curse God and die, and his three friend's repeated accusations of his sin's consequences.

He certainly needed God's reassurance of His majestic power and creation. *Do you know the laws of the universe? Can you use them to regulate the earth? Can you shout to the clouds and make it rain? Can you make lightning appear and cause it to strike as you direct? Who gives intuition to the heart and instinct to the mind? Who is wise enough to count all the clouds? Who can tilt the water jars of heaven?* (Job 38:33-37).

God in His infinite wisdom and love for all His creation created this natural never-ending cycle to support all living things:

Even Solomon with all his wisdom posed this question: *The wind blows south, and then turns north. Around and around it goes, blowing in circles. Rivers run into the sea, but the sea is never full. Then the water returns again to the rivers and flows out again to the sea* (Ecclesiastes 1:6-7).

God's "merry-go-round" never stops!

Chapter 9: Hung Upon Nothing

How would you hold a three-hundred- and sixteen-million-ton ball? The estimated weight of our world. Watch out! Don't let it fall on your toe.

If you're going to suspend it in our Milky Way with 100 thousand million stars, better have some astronomical super structures to hold it up.

A plethora of historical myths propose earth support systems:

1. Ancient Norse religion said: four dwarfs hold up the four corners of the earth. They must have started out as giants.
2. In Shintoism, the god of wind, Shine-Tsu-Hiko, holds it up.
3. Mayans believed it was four gods, the Bacabs, supporting it.
4. Japanese Ainu people described the world as a vast ocean resting on the backbone of a trout that creates the surging of the tides each day by sucking in the ocean and spewing it out. What a job!
5. In Greek mythology, Atlas was forced to support the earth after fighting unsuccessfully against Zeus. Back problems for sure.
6. Iroquois, Hindu, and Gabrielino Indian religions, believed turtles supported the earth. A slow-moving earth, no doubt. Would anyone want the careers these dwarfs, gods and animals had? They must have had tag teams of trout, fish, turtles, and gods.

We know gravitational force holds the earth in place. "Gravity is the force that pulls us to the surface of the Earth, and keeps the planets in orbit around the Sun."[15]

Without the scientific knowledge and equipment available today, who could have even imagined an unsupported earth? Imaginations ran wild.

---

[15] https://www.esa.int/Science_Exploration/Space_Science/The_fundamental_forces_of_nature

Yet the Bible declared almost 4,000 years ago that the earth is not suspended on anything: *God... hangs the earth on nothing* (Job 26:7b).

How amazing, a sphere the size and weight of our earth does not have a gargantuan support system. We're just a tiny speck among zillions of other specks with sizes and weights way beyond ours.

Our God is beyond amazing! He holds everything together. *And He Himself existed and is before all things, and in Him all things hold together. [His is the controlling, cohesive force of the universe]* (Colossians 1:17 AMP).

There's no better support system than the one and only true God of the universe.

What do you hang your hope of afterlife on? Hopefully, it's not hung on nothing.

Chapter 10: Flat or Round World

Believe it or not, an organization of "flat earthers" exists. They insist the earth is flat, not round. Everyone else has been duped by a conspiracy theory. We live in a world of conspiracy theories.

Michael Marshall, project director of a UK charity states, "the whole purpose of our charity is to promote science to challenge pseudoscience." *Scientific American* magazine records his findings on flat earthers. He mentions a very well-educated friend's sister who holds this flat earth belief.[16]

A November 2019 CNN report tells of a third annual Flat Earth International Conference. It was held at an Embassy Suites hotel in suburban Dallas, Texas, and attended by approximately 600 followers.[17]

The Bible said the earth was round, not flat, almost four thousand years ago. *God sits above the **circle** of the earth* (Isaiah 40:22).

The Hebrew word in question is *khûg* (חוּג), which is also found in Job 22:14 where, in many Bible versions, it is translated 'vault.' For example, the New American Standard Bible reads, *He walks on the vault of heaven.* Clearly *vault* carries the sense of something three-dimensional and is given as the primary meaning of *khûg* in the well-known *Brown-Driver-Briggs Hebrew and English Lexicon*.

In modern Hebrew, a sphere is denoted by *khûg*, along with *kaddur*, *galgal*, and *mazzal*.[2] In Arabic (another Semitic language), *kura* means ball and is the word used in the Van Dyck-Boustani Arabic Bible (1865) to translate *khûg* in Isaiah 40:22.[18]

Since God created the earth and everything in it, it makes sense that He would know the shape of the earth.

Has anyone fell off the edge of a flat earth? Front page news for sure.

---

[16] https://www.scientificamerican.com/podcast/episode/flat-earthers-what-they-believe-and-why/

[17] https://www.cnn.com/2019/11/16/us/flat-earth-conference-conspiracy-theories-scli-intl

[18] https://creation.com/isaiah-40-22-circle-sphere

There is controversy over the word "circle" or "khug." Some say it simply means "circle" not "sphere." The Voice, a Christian publication, had an article entitled *The Circle of the Earth: Translation and Meaning in Isaiah 40:22*. It quotes, "Some people, for various reasons, take 'the circle of the earth' in Isaiah 40:22 to be a reference to a spherical earth. This would mean that the ancient Israelites of the eighth century BC knew that the earth was spherical and not flat."[19] What a sad commentary to discount the supernatural ability of God to reveal scientific facts about his creation to His scribes. Writers and people who had no way of knowing the facts.

Be careful what you base your beliefs on. Especially when it comes to the inherent Word of God.

Is the earth flat or round? What's the shape of planets and stars? Do you believe God, our creator, or the "flat earthers?"

---

[19] http://www.crivoice.org/circle.html

Chapter 11: A Different Let it Snow

Snow can be enticing. Unless you have to drive in it or shovel it. Here's some snow facts:

- Each winter in the U.S. at least one septillion snow crystals fall from the sky. A one with twenty-four zeros...1,000,000,000,000,000,000,000,000!
- In 1921, over six feet of snow fell within twenty-four hours in Silver Lake, Colorado.
- In 2007, 8,962 people plopped down in North Dakota snow, waggled their arms and legs and made snow angels.
- "Exactly 5,834 snow fighters came together to exchange frozen barrages to create the largest snowball fight in the world on January 12, 2013."

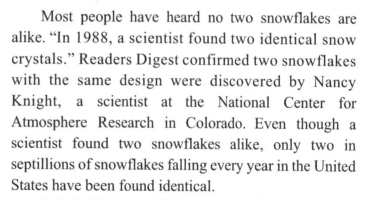

Most people have heard no two snowflakes are alike. "In 1988, a scientist found two identical snow crystals." Readers Digest confirmed two snowflakes with the same design were discovered by Nancy Knight, a scientist at the National Center for Atmosphere Research in Colorado. Even though a scientist found two snowflakes alike, only two in septillions of snowflakes falling every year in the United States have been found identical.

Job 38:22a asks, *"Have you visited the storehouses of the snow?"* (American Standard Version) says *"treasures of the snow."* What's a treasure? "Something precious of great value." God's snow workshop must be incredulous! Septillions of snowflakes, each with its unique design. God didn't say "Oops!" when a couple of twin snowflakes fell. He was just seeing if we were paying attention. How more precious God's children are to Him than His snowflakes! *See how very much our Father loves us, for he calls us his children, and that is what we are!* (1 John 3:1a)

Creator of the *Compound Interest* science blog, Andy Brunning, has painstakingly catalogued thirty-five different types of snowflakes. They are designated as column, plane, rimed, germs, and irregular plus a few combinations of all of them.

Are we the only mammals to enjoy a good snowball fight? Japanese macaques, known as "snow monkeys," have been observed making and playing with balls of snow. Young macaques enjoy stealing each other's snowballs, then battling to retrieve them.

Snow is comprised of ninety to ninety-five percent trapped air. It's a great insulator. This is the reason many animals burrow deep into the snow during winter in order to hibernate. It's also the reason igloos, using only body heat to warm them, can be 100 degrees warmer inside than outside.

"The largest recorded snowflake was fifteen inches wide and eight inches thick. It fell at Fort Keogh, Montana, in January of 1887." Though supporting evidence is limited, the Guinness World Records book lists this as the largest snowflake. What a headache it could have caused.

"Perhaps the most astonishing place to ever receive snow is Death Valley, California. One of the hottest places on Earth, with surface temperatures reaching 120° Fahrenheit, it's not the place you might expect to see snow. But it's happened several times, most recently in December 2008. The Sahara Desert is synonymous with things hot and dry. But it has occasionally seen the exact opposite weather. As recently as 2016, snow landed on this sandy desert floor."

"Chionophobia," is an intense fear of snow, a surprisingly common phobia. The sufferer can obsess over weather reports, stay inside at the slightest hint of snow, or suffer panic attacks when facing snowy weather.[4]

Snow is fascinating. Songs like "I'm Dreaming of a White Christmas" and "Winter Wonderland" remind us of wishful nostalgic thoughts. The anticipation of building a snowman or a snow fort, making snow angels, winning a snowball fight, and sledding, tubing, or skiing down slopes remains the quest of many.

One of my most memorable events was being pulled up a Horn Mountain, Colorado ski slope on a T-bar. Laying on a huge inner tube with a partner, with another tube around our feet, we reached the top, and would race to the adjacent slope, belly flop on our tubes, and zip headlong down the slope. Tuber trains holding each other's legs never arrived intact at the bottom.

May God's forgiveness fall on each of us like snow: *"Come now, let's settle this," says the* LORD. *Though your sins are like scarlet, I will make them as white as snow"* (Isaiah 1:18a).

Let it snow. Let it snow. Let it snow.

Chapter 12: Missing Evolutionary Links

Where did we come from? How did we get here? What or who started it? Did we come from apes? Where are all the links? Who knows?

For centuries, scientists, historians, philosophers, and theologians have searched for and proposed answers to these questions.

All From One

You may hear big terms like mutualism, commensalism, symbiosis, or symbiogenesis from scientists. These words are used to explain how different species of living organisms interacted, had common features or functions, and eventually evolved from one species into another. "Biologist, Lynn Margulis, famous for her work on endosymbiosis, contends that symbiosis is a major driving force behind evolution. She considers Darwin's notion of evolution, driven by competition, to be incomplete and claims that evolution is strongly based on cooperation, interaction, and mutual dependence among organisms."[20]

To get every living organism from one organism seems an insurmountable assignment. One requiring unending eons of time and an unfathomable myriad of changes and intermediate stages of evolution. The next chapter addresses many problems in any evolutionary theory.

---

[20] (http://en.wikipedia.org/wiki/Symbiosis)

How About Us

How humans evolved should be a priority. Evolutionists propose our origin from monkeys and apes. There's been an ongoing search for links between the two. If our origin is found in apes, there should be a plethora of progressive links between the two. Where are they?

Some of the proposed missing "ape-men" have included: The Neanderthal Man (1829/1848), The Cro-Magnon Man (1868), Pithecanthropus Erectus or Java Man (1891), Lucy (1974), and the Turkana Boy (1984) The chart below pictures a supposed progression:

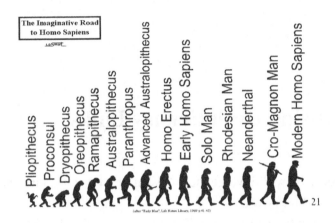

"The entire story of H. erectus (Homo Erectus) is essentially built on about 300 very fragmentary fossils. The majority of these are nothing more than partial skulls, teeth, and broken bones. The only nearly complete H. erectus fossil is Turkana Boy, whose post-cranial skeleton was found to be nearly identical to modern humans."[22]

Mutants Galore

Links between aquatic and land mammals list weird names like: Indohyus, Pakicetidae, Ambulocetidae, Remingtonocetidae, Protocetidae, Basilosauridae, Dorudontinae, and most recently Tiktaalik roseae. From land mammals to birds, we find: Archaeopteryx (from dinosaurs) and Liaoningornis.

Going from one cell to all the different existing species would require a huge number of mutations. These would be unusual, and sometimes, weird changes from the norm. Also, an ongoing process of "transmutations," changing from one species to a totally different species, would be necessary. This would require a myriad of mutations and transmutations.

When considering the more obvious mutations in humans and animals, they are usually harmful, rarely beneficial, and often fatal. If the mutant does not die at birth, its life span is usually drastically shortened.

---

[21] "Unmasking Evolution: The Resource Book" by Laurence D Smart (Creative Commons Attribution-NonCommercial-NoDerivs 3.0 Unported License (http://creativecommons.org/licenses/by-nc-nd/3.0/).
[22] (https://www.icr.org/article/homo-erectus-the-ape-man-that-wasnt)

In humans, examples include downs syndrome and Parkinson's. Other genetic disorders caused by the mutation of a single gene include cystic fibrosis, sickle cell anemia, Tay-Sachs disease, phenylketonuria, and color-blindness, among many others.[23]

"Dogat"

"Dogat" is an example of a supposed transmutation. When I was in college, the Miami Herald newspaper ran a front-page article entitled, "Dogat." A picture of a weird looking "part dog/part cat" accompanied the story.

This 1970 newspaper article was published throughout the United States. A pet store owner in England, Roy Tutt, said he bred a dog and a cat, resulting in his "Dogat." He said it had characteristics of both breeds. Tutt said sometimes it ate dog food, and other times cat food. No surprise. A dog will eat better tasting cat food rather than most dog food. If a cat gets hungry enough, it will eat dog food.

What was really unique and weird was Roy saying sometimes it barked and sometimes it meowed.

The sad and truthful part about all this came a few weeks later. Although, thousands of people read the initial article, very few saw or read the small follow-up article in a back section of newspapers. This was reported a hoax. The pet store owner discovered a weird looking animal and passed it off as a cat-dog mix. Wanting some free publicity, he concocted this deceiving story.[24]

Probably many who read the first article, promote this as a proof for the existence of transmutations between animals.

Links to the Max

Let's use some logic here. If all species of living organisms originated from one original cell or a Big Bang, then there would not be missing links between any species. There would be millions or billions of links between all different life forms. Fossil records would be saturated with intermediate stages.

If humans came from apes, there should be a 95% ape/5% man, 75% ape/25% man, 50% ape/50% man, 25% ape/75% man, 5% ape/95% man, and a whole bunch in-between. Where are they? A student in one of my science classes posed an interesting, yet puzzling question. "If humans came from apes, then why isn't it happening today?"

The same would apply to all the transmutations necessary between all the different species ever to exist. Can we find a witness?

Don't forget how detrimental mutations are. An abundant plethora of links is not found. They are missing.

---

[23] (https://genetics.thetech.org/about-genetics/mutations-and-disease)

[24] (https://www.newspapers.com/search/#query=Dogat&dr_year=1970-1973&offset=1)

After Their Own Kind

In Genesis 1 God created all life forms repeating the same phrase. Fruit trees and vegetation were created in verses 11 and 12, *their seeds produced plants and trees **of the same kind***. In verses 20 and 21, birds and aquatic life came into existence. Land animals were created in verses 24 and 25. All culminating with the phrase *each producing offspring **of the same kind***.

From the beginning of creation, God made all living organisms to reproduce after their own kind. The Bible verifies this saying, *You can identify them by their fruit. Can you pick grapes from thornbushes, or figs from thistles?* (Matthew 7:16)

Certainly, we see evolutionary changes within a species. But not a change from one species to a totally different species. To submit changes from one species to a totally different species and between all the species ever to exist, takes a lot of unfounded faith.

GIGO

In the same way, we can't get something different coming out of our minds than what we put in. God says, *"What you say flows from what is in your heart"* (Luke 6:45). If we really want to know what a person is like, find out what they think about, *"For as he thinks within himself, so he is."* (Proverbs 23:7 NASB).

It's like the term "GIGO" used in computer technology. You always get out exactly what you put in. "Garbage in, garbage out," or "Good in, good out." We can't watch or hear ungodly things repeatedly, and then expect for godly things to come out of our mouths or do things pleasing to the Lord Jesus. We may be able to guard what we do or say in certain situations or around certain people. But when we feel the freedom to "speak our minds," the real us is revealed. Driving in traffic, playing competitive sports, and getting upset often reveals our mental storehouse.

Ever hear the song that says, *Oh be careful little eyes what you see... Oh be careful little ears what you hear... Oh be careful little feet where you go, for your Father up above is looking down in tender love...Oh be careful little eyes, ears, and feet what you see or hear or where you go?*

God commands us, *"And whatever you do or say, do it as a representative of the Lord Jesus, giving thanks through him to God the Father"* (Colossians 3:17). He gets more specific in Ephesians 4:29 (NASB): *"Let no unwholesome word proceed from your mouth, but only such a word as is good for edification according to the need of the moment, so that it will give grace to those who hear."* Those are some of the greatest challenges I know.

Oh, the wonder of God's creations! He doesn't leave any missing links.

Chapter 13: Other Evolutionary Problems—Something from Nothing?

There is a huge problem with evolutionary theories stating all life forms came from one cell, the Big Bang, eternal inflation, or an oscillating universe. Where, when, and how did the first cell or stuff originate? No matter what theory proposed or believed, this question is tantamount.

The First Law of Thermodynamics, also called The Law of Conservation of Mass or Energy, poses a major problem. It states *matter cannot be created or destroyed.* Even if one cell, protein, or a small singularity could be created from some primeval soup with the right chemicals coming together under the right conditions, how did the necessary stuff get there? How about a Big Bang creating the universe and everything in it? Where and from what did the big colliding bodies come from? You cannot get something from nothing. God knew this law before science discovered it.

Everything in our world and universes consists of one or more atoms of one or more elements. A magic wand cannot be waved and *Poof!* atoms with protons, electrons, and neutrons appear. If so, where and from what did someone get a magic wand?

BIGGER, Better, Best

Evolutionists believe all life forms evolved from simple to complex, a one celled protozoa, all the way to man. Evolving life forms became better and better. This occurred through processes of natural selection and survival of the fittest.

The second Law of Thermodynamics or Law of Entropy basically says, "As energy is transferred or transformed, more and more of it is wasted." This Second Law also states, "There is a natural tendency of any isolated system to degenerate into a more disordered state."[25]

---

[25] (https://www.livescience.com/50941-second-law-thermodynamics.html)

Things left on their own tend to randomness. They don't get better and better. They get worse and worse. Especially if there is no means of maintenance.

We see this happening all around us. Wine and cheese left alone may get better with age, but not much else does. Even wine and cheese get moldy when exposed to air for any length of time. If consistent, nurturing care is not given the human body, animals, and plants, they don't get better, they get worse. They wilt and die. Even with good attention and care, over time, our bodies and living things "fall apart." One of my uncles says, "Getting old is not for sissies." I'm experiencing this truth.

God told Adam and Eve death would be one consequence of their disobedience. *But the LORD God warned him, "You may freely eat the fruit of every tree in the garden—except the tree of the knowledge of good and evil. If you eat its fruit, you are sure to die* (Genesis 2:16-17).

Even God's creations would suffer the same destiny. *"Long ago you laid the foundation of the earth and made the heavens with your hands. They will perish, but you remain forever; they will wear out like old clothing. You will change them like a garment and discard them. But you are always the same; you will live forever"* (Psalm 102:25-27).

Bigger, better, best—if only we'd get better until we're laid to rest.

The Pursuit of Time

Evolutionists are always looking for older things, giving more and more time to explain, a puzzling evolutionary process. It is an ominous task explaining how everything in our world and universe got here from a single cell or a big bang. Even with millions or billions of years it seems an impossible task.

The world-wide flood recorded in the Bible and most ancient civilizations provides an answer. The Grand Canyon and like structures, sediment, and coal formations could occur in a short period of time. Imagine the entire world covered with water, including the highest mountains. If one gallon of water weighs a little more than eight pounds, the pressure exerted by billions of gallons of water with a depth as high as the tallest mountain would be a Herculean burden.

The flood also gives insight into how dinosaur and human footprints have been found in the same geological strata. Even life forms from different geological ages have been discovered in the same strata. A world-wide flood would create the largest centrifuge ever. A shaking, swirling, agitating separator like no other.

No Sex

Even if you could somehow defy scientific law and come up with the first stuff for the first cell coming from nothing, problems still remain.

How would the first cell reproduce? A mitotic asexual (without male and female) reproduction would be the only option. One cell replicates and divides, forming two cells. Two cells become four. Four soon are eight, and eventually, out pops a human. Just think, the average adult human being has 7 times 10^{27} atoms in their body. Do the math, seven with twenty-seven zeroes behind it, or seven billion, billion, billion. Even if you want smaller numbers, the approximated number of cells in an average human is around 70 trillion.

The arduous question is how, why, and when did sexual cells appear? Evolutionists may say many organisms reproduce both sexually and asexually. It does not answer the how, why, and when questions.

God puts it simply when creating human beings, "*He created them male and female, and he blessed them and called them 'human'*" (Genesis 5:2). Even the animals taken into the ark were by twos, male and female. "*A male and female of each kind entered, just as God had commanded Noah. Then the LORD closed the door behind them*" (Genesis 7:16).

It takes a lot more blind faith to believe everything got here from one original cell or a Big Bang than to believe God created all basic life forms and species.

After Their Own Kind

If you don't believe in one, and only one, supreme God as creator, you must come up with an explanation of how everything got here. I don't like saying "Good luck," because with God there's no such thing as luck. "*For He gives His sunlight to both the evil and the good, and he sends rain on the just and the unjust alike*" (Matthew 5:45). "*Whatever is good and perfect is a gift coming down to us from God our Father, who created all the lights in the heavens. He never changes or casts a shifting shadow* (James 1:17). God is in control of everything. He either brings or allows everything coming our way.

Even a theory like "Theistic Evolution," stating that God created the first cell or stuff and then everything evolved, does not answer all the problems and questions of how everything could possibly come from one cell or a Big Bang! It may seem to obey the First Law of Thermodynamics, but not the second.

The Bible clearly answers the questions and problems these theories cannot answer:

Genesis

1:11: God creates plants, trees and vegetation, "*Their seeds produced plants and trees **of the same kind**.*"

1:20-21 - God creates aquatic life and birds, "*…each producing offspring **of the same kind**.*"

1:24 - God creates all land animals, "*…each producing offspring **of the same kind**.*"

We certainly see this in the reproduction of human beings. Everything God created reproduced after its own kind/species.

According to the Biblical account, God/Jesus created everything. Speaking of Jesus, the Word, God in the flesh: "*In the beginning the Word already existed. The Word was with God, and the Word was God. He existed in the beginning with God. God created everything through him, and nothing was created except through him*" (John 1:1-3).

Evolution obviously happens within a given species. "Survival of the fittest" often occurs. The individuals best suited to their environment are the ones who usually survive longer and better over those less fit to live in the same environment.

"Adaptation" takes place within every species. Individuals within the same species will usually adapt to the environment they live in. Some, or many, may adapt to a changing environment. Those who adapt most efficiently are most likely to survive longer than those who don't adapt or do not adapt as well as others.

Although many mutations are not beneficial, but are harmful, shorten life spans, or can be fatal, some can be beneficial. Many individuals within a certain species are much different than those in past civilizations and environments. Examples include modern day dogs, cats, many other animals, and even humans.

Through mutations, adaptation, and survival of the fittest, individuals within a species have evolved and continue to evolve. I again mention a student asking, "If man came from apes, why isn't it still happening today?" Got a verifiable answer?

When we look around at the world and universe we live in, how can one help but be amazed at the complexity, gazillion varieties, uniqueness, and beauty in living organisms. Look within the human body. To believe this all came into being and evolved from a primeval soup or stellar body leaves one clinging to a speculative faith. To believe in a creator God with unequaled power and wisdom who spoke it all into existence is a more credible and plausible persuasion.

"No hay problema." No problems man. God left no missing links in his chain of creation.

Chapter 14: Wonderfully Made

How can anyone look at the infinite number and variety of plants and animals in our world and believe it happened through an evolutionary process?

The Lord God who created the universe and everything in it wants us to see how magnificent, unique, and beautiful His creations are. "*Just ask the animals, and they will teach you. Ask the birds of the sky, and they will tell you. Speak to the earth, and it will instruct you. Let the fish in the sea speak to you. For they all know that my disaster has come from the hand of the LORD. For the life of every living thing is in his hand, and the breath of every human being* (Job 12:7-10). All of God's creation proclaims His magnificence. And Job proclaimed this message after experiencing more catastrophes than most people will experience in a lifetime.

"*O LORD, what a variety of things you have made! In wisdom you have made them all. The earth is full of your creatures. Here is the ocean, vast and wide, teeming with life of every kind, both large and small*" (Psalm 104:24-25).

Having taught Marine Science in high school, I'm not only amazed by the countless magnitude of different species in the ocean, but its beauty and uniqueness is mystifying. "…scientists estimate that 91 percent of ocean species have yet to be classified, and that 95 percent of the ocean remains unexplored."[26]

Over 17,000 species thrive in the deep sea where no light penetrates the ocean waves? How amazing is God's creation?

"Currently, scientists have named and successfully classified around 1.5 million species. It is estimated that there are as little as two million to as many as fifty million more species that have not yet been found and/or have been incorrectly classified."[277]

"*Look at the lilies and how they grow. They don't work or make their clothing, yet Solomon in all his glory was not dressed as beautifully as they are* (Luke 12:27). Even flowers portray a

---

[26] https://oceanservice.noaa.gov/facts/ocean-species.html
[27] https://marinebio.org/creatures/facts

magnificent beauty only God could orchestrate. Maybe it's the reason most women love to be given a bouquet. It's one of the most common gifts for special occasions and showing care for ones suffering from an illness or having died.

Speaking of His universe and stars, God proclaims: *"Look up into the heavens. Who created all the stars? He brings them out like an army, one after another, calling each by its name. Because of his great power and incomparable strength, not a single one is missing."* (Isaiah 40:26) *"The heavens proclaim the glory of God. The skies display his craftsmanship."* (Psalm 19:1).

Beyond Comparison

The human body is one of the most complex, amazing, and brilliant of God's creations. *"Thank you for making me so wonderfully complex! Your workmanship is marvelous—how well I know it."* (Psalm 139:14). What a body! One hundred thousand miles of blood vessels, trillions of bacteria, and produces twenty-five million cells every second. Skin, our largest organ, helps keep us at the right temperature, helps with touch and sensation, allows movement without restriction, and heals and regenerates constantly.[28]

Summarizing all of His creation God states: *"Then God looked over all he had made, and he saw that it was very good!"* (Genesis 1:31a). *"He has made everything beautiful in his time..."* (Ecclesiastes 3:11a KJV). At the end of each day of creation the Bible records God saying what He created was "good." But after He created man, He says everything He created was "very good!" (Genesis 1:31)

The Ultimate

But the most important reason for all of God's creation is culminated in His coming to earth as Jesus Christ for the express purpose of redeeming all of mankind. By His death on the cross He paid for all the sins of all mankind. By His resurrection everyone who accepts His payment for all their sin and places their trust completely in Him receive His guarantee of eternal life.

In John 6:47 (NKJV) Jesus put it simply in a few words: *"Most assuredly, I say to you, he who believes in Me has everlasting life."*

---

[28] (https://www.newsweek.com/mind-blowing-facts-about-your-body-human-1638872)

PROPHETICAL FACTS

Chapter 15: Satan's Killer Bruise

We've all had bruises. They hurt. What causes a bruise? Dead blood cells come to the surface of the skin due to some physical trauma from a blow or injury. Over time the dead blood cells are absorbed and the bruise disappears.

One medical report verifies an unusual case, where in a rare syndrome, a bruise could mean death. Wiskott-Aldrich syndrome turns even minor injuries into grave emergencies.[29]

A Genesis 3:15 prophesy talks about a bruise causing death. God speaking to the Serpent, (Satan) who deceived Eve, exclaims, **"***And I will put enmity between you and the woman, And between your seed and her Seed; He shall bruise your head, And you shall bruise His heel***"** (NKJV). How would a human offspring from the seed of Eve bruise the head of Satan, giving him a deadly blow?

An interesting aside was pointed out by Del Tackett in his Engagement Project. He asked the question how a woman would have a reproductive seed. Only men have a seed for procreation. Women have eggs awaiting fertilization by the male seed. This parallels the Messianic prophecy of God coming to earth as Jesus through a virgin birth. *"All right then, the Lord himself will give you the sign. Look! The virgin will conceive a child! She will give birth to a son and will call him Immanuel (which means 'God is with us')"* (Isaiah 7:14). Eve's "seed" was the miraculous one provided by God alone. A sign unlike any other.

Hebrews 2:14b-15 gives the answer to Jesus giving Satan a deadly blow: *"the Son also became flesh and blood. For only as a human being could He die, and only by dying could He break the power of the devil, who had the power of death. Only in this way could He set free all who have lived their lives as slaves to the fear of dying."* By the death of the Lord Jesus Christ on a rugged

---

[29] (https://abcnews.go.com › Health › Wellness › story)

cross, Satan's head was crushed. The goal of Satan, to deceive the world and have them ultimately join him in an eternal hell separated forever from the one and only holy God, was defeated.

How was Jesus' "heel bruised?" I'm sure Satan jumped up and down thinking the death of Jesus was a victory for him. His goal to deceive all mankind would not be hindered by a dead god here on earth. But his elation was a brief three-day celebration.

A bruise to the heel does not cause death like the deadly bruise Jesus dealt to Satan. The resurrection of Jesus Christ assured all born-gain believers of their victory over a physical death and guaranteed resurrection to an eternal life in heaven with a perfect Savior. Only a perfect one, Jesus, could die and pay for all the sin of everyone. Thereby, He provided salvation forever to anyone and everyone who accepts and trusts His gift by faith alone in Christ alone.

Look at God's promise to every Christian: "*And when you believed in Christ, he identified you as his own - by giving you the Holy Spirit, whom he promised long ago. The Spirit is God's guarantee that he will give us the inheritance he promised and that he has purchased us to be his own people. He did this so we would praise and glorify him*" (Ephesians 1:13b-14).

The greatest question ever asked is this: have you received eternal life? A gift freely available to everyone by Christ's killer bruise to Satan?

Chapter 16: Virgin or Young Woman

Isaiah 7:14 (AMP) prophesied, *Therefore the Lord Himself will give you a sign: Listen carefully, the virgin will conceive and give birth to a son, and she will call his name Immanuel (God with us).*

Most Bible translations use the word "virgin" in this verse.

The Revised Standard Bible (RSV) caused a controversy when it translated Isaiah 7:14 using the phrase "young woman" instead of "virgin." This was believed to be a covert attack on Christ's virgin birth. Today, many Evangelicals refuse to use the RSV or the NRSV bibles because of this verse alone.

A preface to the information in the next paragraph: How the word "virgin" is translated should be the litmus test in determining which version to use and base the Bible's validity upon.

Choosing which Bible version to use should be predicated on the clarity of its most important message and theme: salvation.

Raymond E. Brown (an American Catholic priest, a prominent biblical scholar and author of some 40 books) said, "Isaiah 7:14 has become a litmus test for Bible translations, such that any Bible that does not translate Isaiah 7:14 with the word 'virgin' is suspect and this is a tragedy for many reasons. The first is that academic theology primarily uses the NRSV for English translations and has caused Evangelicals to distrust any theologian who uses NRSV (or RSV) and therefore has caused evangelicals to distance themselves from credible theology. The second is this litmus test indicates that evangelicals prefer Bible translations that are biased towards their ideologies. All Bible translations are ultimately commentaries upon the original sources, so none are free from bias. This is unavoidable. However, it is deceptive to intentionally translate a Bible contrary to its sources to make it align with one's own agendas, especially when biased Bibles are toted as the only correct translation and used for subversive measures to attack those who do not use a specific English translation. Using Isaiah 7:14 as a litmus test for rejecting the RSV, NRSV, NJB or any

Bible translation that uses the phrase 'young woman' instead of 'virgin' may be symptomatic of a cultic and biased approach to theology and the Bible." [30]

This passage, quoted from Postbarthian.com, illustrates the problem when something in the Bible is taken out of its context. Yes, the Hebrew word for "virgin" in Isaiah 7:14 is "alma." "Alma" is the Hebrew word for "young woman." But look at the context of this verse.

This verse is a Messianic prophecy. It begins by stating *Therefore the Lord Himself will give you a sign.* A "young woman" having a child would not be a "sign from God." This event happens somewhere in the world every second. "There are about four babies born each second worldwide."[31]

Plus, this is not going to be just another baby. Even though most babies born are special and the cutest thing ever to their parents and grandparents, this was going to be a "one-of-a-kind" baby. The end of the verse tells what this baby's name would be, *Immanuel.* The meaning of the Hebrew word "Immanuel" is "God with us." This baby would be the one and only true God. Now there's a sign like no other. Not only would this be God coming to earth as a baby, but in a way that defied all the laws of childbirth, through a virgin.

In the same book of the Bible, Isaiah prophesied this child, God's Son, would be God himself: *"For a child is born to us, a son is given to us. The government will rest on his shoulders. And he will be called: Wonderful Counselor, **Mighty God, Everlasting Father**, Prince of Peace"* (Isaiah 9:6).

Jesus Christ Himself made it crystal clear He was and is God. Right after He said in John 14:6, *"I am the way, and the truth, and the life. No one comes to the Father except through me,"* He said, *"If you had known me, you would have known my Father also. From now on you do know Him and have seen Him"* (John 14:7). Philip asked Jesus to show them the Father and they would be satisfied. Jesus must have shaken His head, and in amazement asked: *"Have I been with you so long, and you still do not know me, Philip? Whoever has seen me has seen the Father. How can you say, 'Show us the Father?'"*

Again, in John10:30, Jesus got right to the point, *"I and the Father are one."* Don't ask me to explain the Trinity, how the only true God is three distinct persons in one person. It's a God thing. Without a doubt, Jesus Christ was, is, and always will be fully God.

John 1:1-5 nails it. *"In the beginning the Word already existed. The Word was with God, and the Word was God. He existed in the beginning with God. God created everything through him, and nothing was created except through him. The Word gave life to everything that was created, and his life brought light to everyone. The light shines in the darkness, and the darkness can never extinguish it."* Jesus, "The Word," "The Light," is the only true God.

Dr. David Jeremiah states, "Jesus was God walking around in a body." He was fully God and fully man. What can we compare him to? Just like the Trinity, there's no comparison.

---

[30] (Postbarthian.com "Virgin or Young Woman in Isaiah 7:14: A Litmus Test for Bible Translations")
[31] (https://www.quora.com/How-many-babies-are-born-a-second.)

Is it just a biased belief saying Jesus was God and born of a virgin, not a young woman? No, it's a miraculous sign unlike any other. God would choose to come to earth as a baby born of a virgin, with the express purpose of providing redemption and salvation for everyone. Eternal life in heaven is freely given to anyone and everyone who accepts His payment for all their sins as their only means of obtaining life everlasting. *"For this is how God loved the world: He gave his one and only Son, so that everyone who believes in him will not perish but have eternal life. God sent his Son into the world not to judge the world, but to save the world through him. There is no judgment against anyone who believes in him. But anyone who does not believe in him has already been judged for not believing in God's one and only Son"* (John 3:16-18).

The miraculous birth of the Lord Jesus Christ. Not just another normal childbirth, a one-of-a-kind virgin birth.

Chapter 17: A Hollywood Jesus

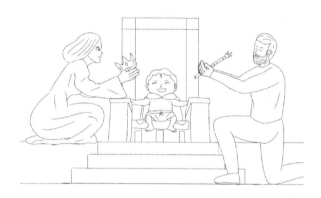

What would Jesus' birth have looked like if orchestrated by Hollywood? I mean, God coming to earth. The most spectacular event ever. Look.

Who would be the producer? Not one, a collaboration of the greatest. Of course, Steven Spielberg, Samuel Goldwyn, Clint Eastwood, Sam Spiegel, and George Lucas would be there. And Brian Grazer would be included. He's been nominated for a total of forty-three Oscars. Couldn't leave out Scott Rudin. At the age of 27, he became president of production at 20th Century Fox. He was the first producer to win an Oscar, Grammy, Emmy, and Tony Award for his productions.

What about the set? Where in the world would God come to earth? How about *The Setai* in Miami Beach, an oasis of tranquility and architectural beauty. There's the luxury hotel, *Taj Diplomatic,* set on six lush acres in the prestigious Diplomatic Enclave in New Delhi, a great choice. The *Inter-Continental Bora Bora Resort and Thalasso Spa* in French Polynesia, offering private villas over the water and an exclusive private beach at $933 per night, should be on the list. Can't leave out *Hotel Wailea,* Maui, Hawaii, set on fifteen tropical acres overlooking three Hawaiian islands. Or *Tambo del Inka,* a Luxury Collection Resort and Spa in the Sacred Valley of Peru. Tough choice, to pick just one. Since God is omnipresent, we could have Him in more than one place at the same time. Maybe even all those places. A box office hit no doubt.

Who to cast? Robert Redford would play Joseph. A young Elizabeth Taylor as Mary. One more addition to a long list of husbands. Golden-haired Macaulay Culkin makes a perfect baby Jesus. The shepherds would include Tom Hanks, Sean Penn, and Denzel Washington. Wise guys from afar consist of Jim Carrey, Adam Sandler, and Eddie Murphy. Don't forget the innkeeper. How about Bill Murray?

Of course, there would be a sequel thirty years later ... *Superstar Jesus Saves the World.* Tom Cruise would play the part.

But it didn't happen like that. God, in His omnipotence and omniscience, chose an illogical scenario.

At the time of Jesus' birth, there were two Bethlehem's in Israel, Bethlehem Zebulun and Bethlehem Ephratah. If we were to choose between the two, we'd choose Zebulun. Why? It was a lot bigger, a city, instead of a village. Also, Zebulun was right around the corner from where Joseph and Mary lived in Nazareth. Ephratah, on the other hand, was some 80-90 miles over rugged terrain. A foot trip requiring four to seven days, especially for a close to nine months pregnant Mary. Many pictures show Mary riding on a donkey. Scripture does not substantiate this. Bouncing on a donkey probably wouldn't have been Mary's choice.

God prophesied in Micah 5:2 (NKJV), *"But you, Bethlehem Ephratah, though you are little among the thousands of Judah, yet out of you shall come forth to Me, the One to be Ruler in Israel, whose goings forth are from of old, from-everlasting."*

At least we would put baby Jesus up in the best hotel in Bethlehem. Luke 2:7 tells us, *"She gave birth to her firstborn son. She wrapped him snugly in strips of cloth and laid him in a manger, because there was no lodging available for them."* Not only no hotel, but wrapped in cloth, not a royal robe? And a manger, an animal food trough, instead of an elaborate throne crib? Does this make any sense?

Isn't it amazing that every baby born is the cutest little thing? Certainly, Jesus would be the best-looking baby ever born. He would grow up to be the most handsome man alive. He would stand out in any crowd. Of course, *Entertainment* magazine would vote Him as the best-looking guy in the world, for three years running.

His popularity would be astounding, more than anyone before him or after him.

Here's the prophetical account of what the Messiah Jesus would look like and his popularity: *"My servant grew up in the LORD's presence like a tender green shoot, like a root in dry ground. There was nothing beautiful or majestic about his appearance, nothing to attract us to him. He was despised and rejected - a man of sorrows, acquainted with deepest grief. We turned our backs on him and looked the other way. He was despised, and we did not care,"* quotes Isaiah 53:2-3.

What would his role in life be? Without question, he would be King Jesus, the superman hero, to deliver his people Israel from bondage. Isaiah continues God's illogical prophetic narrative, *"But he was pierced for our rebellion, crushed for our sins. He was beaten so we could be whole. He was whipped so we could be healed. All of us, like sheep, have strayed away. We have left God's paths to follow our own. Yet the* LORD *laid on him the sins of us all"* (Isaiah 53:5,6).

Another proof of the Bible being the Word of God, radically set apart from man's ideas or logic. Even though God used men to pen His words, men of their own volition would not have written the birth of Jesus the way God did.

"My thoughts are nothing like your thoughts, says the LORD. *And my ways are far beyond anything you could imagine. For just as the heavens are higher than the earth, so my ways are higher than your ways and my thoughts higher than your thoughts"* (Isaiah 55:8-9).

O, what love, what humility. Definitely a far cry from a Hollywood Jesus.

Chapter 18: Tortured to Death

Every now and then a cut, a trickle of blood, and a bruise here and there find their way to my body. I often don't even know how I got them. Sometimes not even feeling any pain. Certainly not experiencing torture.

Ever see a picture of Jesus on a cross with some blood trickles coming from his crown of small thorns? And not much else showing any signs of trauma?

I'll never forget a riveting account I heard years ago of the unimaginable torture Jesus endured for you, me, and everyone else. A much more vivid description than even recorded in Isaiah 53:5-6: "*But he was pierced for our rebellion, crushed for our sins. He was beaten so we could be whole. He was whipped so we could be healed. All of us, like sheep, have strayed away. We have left God's paths to follow our own. Yet the LORD laid on Him the sins of us all.*"

The message was at a secluded retreat on the snow slopes of Horn Mountain, Colorado (a mountain higher than the more well-known Pikes Peak). I was with my college group from church. We were tubing on huge inner tubes down ski slopes. What a blast!

But the most memorable experience was shared with us by Thor Hagen. A retired professional wrestler, who had an inner-city ministry in Kansas City, Missouri. He had done extensive research on the events preceding Christ's crucifixion.

Those attending his ministry were often turned off to religions and the Bible. Many were from street gangs. He would not use Bibles at all. Instead, in everyday language, he told Bible stories based on extensive study and research.

The first thing he mentioned was the fact of Roman soldiers being masters in the art of torture. They were typically huge, burly, stocky specimens of guerilla warriors.

The Bible describes the violent punches inflicted on Jesus saying they "buffeted" him (Matthew 26:67). Thor mentioned they were pounding him with closed fists, even in his face. He said the professional wrestling he did was nothing like what is televised nowadays. It was real, not fake. He often saw wrestlers who had faces so beaten, swollen, and disfigured from being repeatedly punched so hard, they were almost unrecognizable. Jesus was no exception. *"But many were amazed when they saw him. His face was so disfigured he seemed hardly human, and from his appearance, one would scarcely know he was a man."* This is an Isaiah 52:14 Messianic prophecy.

Previously reading the account of Jesus being whipped, I imagined him hamstrung with hands stretched up and tied like in Western cowboy movies. A leather whip placing welted stripes across his back. Roman soldiers had a much better torture practice. Their subject was laid and strapped to a post elevated by two stumps. The full force of the whip from an over hand power assault ripped and shredded the back of the one being tortured. They probably roared with laughter at his raw and bleeding back.

Their whips were scourging weapons. Thick leather was woven with rough pieces of metal and bone. They were appropriately named "scorpions" or "flagrums." Not only was the brute force of these soldiers felt, but Jesus' skin was literally ripped from his body. Excruciating pain wracked his body. No surprise Jesus stumbled and fell under the weight of a huge, probably rugged and splintered, wooden cross on his back. The song, "The Old Rugged Cross," comes to mind.

Jesus was probably flogged at least thirty-nine times. Deuteronomy 25:3 states a criminal should not receive more than forty lashes. As mercenary specialists, the Roman soldiers would give the max. And not being under Jewish law, they may not have stopped at thirty-nine or forty. Some speculate forty lashes could kill a person.

As if all this is not enough torture for any human being to endure, a crown of thorns was placed on Jesus' head. A cruel mockery of his supposed kingship. Not a crown was placed there. Matthew 27:27-30 states how a crown of thorns was placed on his head and then they beat him on the head with rods. The thorns dug deep into his head. His bruised and swollen head was flooded with blood. And then to add insult to injury, they bowed as if to worship this supposed king. What humiliation on top of extreme cruelty!

Can we imagine what it was like to have thorns buried deep into someone's head. When I visited Israel, I saw thorn bushes with six inch or longer thorns. I'm sure they found the longest, sharpest thorns.

But the ultimate torture was a mental one. Mocked as a false king, try to imagine the humiliation resulting from having all your clothes ripped off in public, a thorn crown mocking your dignity, a reed forced into your hand instead of a scepter, and the same ones who have almost beaten you to death bow down acting like they're worshipping you.

Then to top it all off they rear their heads back and spit in your face. Thor told us of repeated taunts and cursing being hurled at him after a match by the ones who hated you, especially when you've beaten their hero. Being dog-tired and beat all he wanted, while walking the long isle to the locker room, was a shower, get home, and sleep as quickly as possible.

He recounted an incident where a little short man kept trying everything he could think of, not only to insult and humiliate him, but to illicit a violent response. When nothing was working, he jumped into the isle blocking Thor's path. When hurled slurs about Thor's mother failed, he threw his head back and spit in his face. Thor said it would have been easier for him to take dozens of beatings. He felt like twisting the nasty head off the little rat. And he could have easily done just that.

Oh, I forgot to describe Thor. Both of my legs could come close to fitting inside Thor's shirt sleeve. He was built like a tank, a tall, monstrous tank. It would be the height of stupidity to mess with him.

There's no record of a word being uttered by Jesus to those torturing and humiliating Him. Utterly amazing! A fulfillment of prophecy. "*He was oppressed and treated harshly, yet he never said a word. He was led like a lamb to the slaughter. And as a sheep is silent before the shearers, he did not open his mouth*" (Isaiah 53:7).

Taunting cries mocked him as King of the Jews who could save himself and come down off the cross. Another song echoes in my mind. "He could have called ten thousand angels to destroy the world and set him free. He could have called ten thousand angels, but He died alone for you and me."

After all this, his response was one of forgiveness. "*Father, forgive them, for they don't know what they are doing*" (Luke 23:34). Forgive them? Look what those bullies have done to you. And for what? He'd done nothing wrong.

The most Amazing Grace in the universe was God coming to earth as Jesus Christ and dying on a cross for the very ones who tortured him to death. "*Now, most people would not be willing to die for an upright person, though someone might perhaps be willing to die for a person who is especially good. But God showed his great love for us by sending Christ to die for us while we were still sinners*" (Romans 5:7-8).

"*He himself is the sacrifice that atones for our sins—and not only our sins but the sins of all the world*" (1 John 2:2).

"Amazing grace how sweet the sound, that saved a wretch like me." He was tortured to death for the worst people in the world.

Chapter 19: One Plus One Plus One Equals One

How in the world can one plus one plus one equal one? Not in this world, but it can in God's.

I've heard it said the word "trinity" is not mentioned once in the Bible, so it must not be true. Many words are not mentioned in the Bible, yet their concepts are clearly mentioned and verified. The words describing God's "omniscience" (all knowing), "omnipresence" (everywhere present), and "omnipotence" (all powerful), are never mentioned in the Bible but are born out in the repeated attributes of the one and only true God. Even divinity, incarnation, monotheism, and rapture are some of many others absent in the Bible, but their absolute validity is described in detail. Even the word "Bible" is not there.

The trinity found in the Bible from its beginning to its end is an incomprehensible fact. How three different persons can exist as one God finds no comparison on earth or anywhere else. Some attempts to explain the trinity include:

- An egg - having three parts, a shell, white, and yoke in one egg.
- Water's different states of matter - liquid, solid, and gas/steam.
- One person being a spouse, a parent, and an individual.

None of these adequately or fully explain the trinity of God. Neither can we compare anything on this earth as being all powerful, everywhere present at the same time, or knowing everything there is to know.

Thank God we can't know and understand everything about God. If we did, would we have as much need for His help, intervention in our lives, or most importantly, His atonement and a salvation? *If God was small enough for my brain to fully understand, He wouldn't be big enough to save me!*"[32]

---

[32] (https://keithferrin.com/simple-explain-trinity/)

God himself tells us it is impossible to understand everything about Him. Isaiah 55:8 proclaims, *"My thoughts are nothing like your thoughts," says the LORD. "And my ways are far beyond anything you could imagine. For just as the heavens are higher than the earth, so my ways are higher than your ways and my thoughts higher than your thoughts"* We are not talking about the differing distance between our "heaven," atmosphere, and the earth, but the plural "heavens." It's amazing. We have never come to the end of our universe through space travel or even better and better telescopes. There are billions of galaxies outside our own. The difference in our thoughts and ways compared to God's is unfathomable and immeasurable.

How do we know there is a trinity? The Bible repeatedly speaks of God the Father, God the Son (Jesus Christ/Yeshua) and God the Holy Spirit. But how do we know they are all one being?

From the beginning of creation one God (Hebrew "El") proclaimed His plurality (Elohim). "'Elohim' is found 2,602 times in the Hebrew Bible (Tanakh, Old Testament). It is not used in the Greek New Testament."[33]

God declares in Genesis 1:26a (ESV), *"Let **us** make man in **our** image, according to **our** likeness."* Why would a monotheistic god use the words *us* and *our*? Who was He talking to?

Genesis 1:1 (AMP) states, *"In the beginning God (Elohim) created [by forming from nothing] the heavens and the earth."* Parallel these verses with John 1, *"In the beginning [before all time] was the Word (Christ), and the Word was with God, and the Word was God Himself. He was [continually existing] in the beginning [co-eternally] with God. All things were made and came into existence through Him; and without Him not even one thing was made that has come into being. In Him was life [and the power to bestow life], and the life was the Light of men."* (John 1:1-4 AMP).

The last Bible quote clearly shows Jesus Christ was God. The ongoing contention of the religious Pharisees and Sadducees of Jesus' day was His claim to be God. *"Jesus said, 'At my Father's direction I have done many good works. For which one are you going to stone me?'"*

They replied, "We're stoning you not for any good work, but for blasphemy! You, a mere man, claim to be God" (John 10:32-33). Obviously, they clearly understood who Jesus said he was. They would accept His performing miracles, but when He forgave people of their sins, they were incensed saying only God could forgive sins. They were correct, it was God in the flesh performing miracles and forgiving sin.

Jesus clearly stated He was God when talking to His disciples. In John 14:6, *"Jesus told him, 'I am the way, the truth, and the life. No one can come to the Father except through me.'"*

Continuing, He said, *"If you had really known me, you would know who my Father is. From now on, you do know him and have seen him!"* Not understanding what Jesus was saying, Philip said, *"Lord, show us the Father, and we will be satisfied."* In amazement, Jesus replies, *"Have I been with you all this time, Philip, and yet you still don't know who I am? Anyone who has seen me has seen the Father! So why are you asking me to show him to you? Don't you believe that I am in the Father and the Father is in me? The words I speak are not my own, but my Father who*

---

[33] (http://www.hebrew-streams.org/works/hebrew/context-elohim.html)

lives in me does his work through me. Just believe that I am in the Father and the Father is in me. Or at least believe because of the work you have seen me do."

Further clarification is given in John 10:30 where Jesus succinctly states, *"The Father and I are one."*

Speaking of Jesus in Colossians 1:15-17 (ESV) Paul wrote: *"Christ is the visible image of the invisible God. He existed before anything was created and is supreme over all creation, for through him God created everything in the heavenly realms and on earth. He made the things we can see and the things we can't see - such as thrones, kingdoms, rulers, and authorities in the unseen world. Everything was created through him and for him. He existed before anything else, and he holds all creation together."* How could Jesus create everything and exist before there was anything if He was not the one true God?

Old Testament prophesies of the coming Messiah substantiate Him being God in the flesh. *"All right then, the Lord himself will give you the sign. Look! The virgin will conceive a child! She will give birth to a son and will call him Immanuel (which means '**God is with us**')"* (Isaiah 7:14).

The same message is echoed in Isaiah 9:6, *"For a child is born to us, a son is given to us. The government will rest on his shoulders. And he will be called: Wonderful Counselor, **Mighty God**, **Everlasting Father**, Prince of Peace."* This prophecy clearly says the coming Messiah would be God, the Father who has always existed and always will exist.

One religion believes Jesus Christ was the "Mighty God," but not the "Almighty God," the Father. What's the next title after "Mighty God" in the previous verse? Who's the Everlasting Father?

Isaiah 53:5-6 prophesied the mission of Jesus Christ. *"But he was pierced for our rebellion, crushed for our sins. He was beaten so we could be whole. He was whipped so we could be healed. All of us, like sheep, have strayed away. We have left God's paths to follow our own. Yet the LORD laid on him the sins of us all."* These prophecies are written in past tense, showing God had already planned these things before they ever happened.

No mortal man, regardless of their miraculous power or righteous living, could die on a cross as the sole atoning payment for the sins of all mankind. *"For everyone has sinned; we all fall short of God's glorious standard"* (Romans 3:23). Only a perfect, sinless God could pay the ultimate price for all sin there would ever be. *"For God made Christ, who never sinned, to be the offering for our sin, so that we could be made right with God through Christ"* (2 Corinthians 5:21).

NIV words it: *"God made him who had no sin to be sin for us, so that in him we might become the righteousness of God."* Christ's sinless righteousness is given everyone who trusts Christ's complete payment for all their sins as their only freeway to a perfect unblemished heaven.

I have heard preachers tell "sinners" they are going to hell. No one will ever go to hell because they are a sinner. We're all sinners and keep on sinning even as God's children. 1 John 2:2 clearly states all sin is paid for. All sin for everyone. *"He himself is the sacrifice that atones for our sin - and not only our sins but the sins of all the world."* The only reason anyone will spend an eternity separated from God in hell is that they refuse or neglect to accept the payment Jesus Christ has made for all their sins as the only means to heaven. *"God saved you by his grace when you believed.*

And you can't take credit for this; it is a gift from God. Salvation is not a reward for the good things we have done, so none of us can boast about it" (Ephesians 2:8-9).

Okay, Jesus Christ is God, but what about the Holy Spirit? Ephesians 4:4-6 uses the word "one" repeatedly: *"For there is **one** body and **one** Spirit, just as you have been called to **one** glorious hope for the future. There is **one** Lord, **one** faith, **one** baptism, **one** God and Father of all, who is over all, in all, and living through all."*

The great commission Jesus gave to His disciples before He returned to heaven uses a singular "name," not "names," when listing the trinity: *"Therefore, go and make disciples of all the nations, baptizing them in the name of the Father and the Son and the Holy Spirit"* (Matthew 28:19). *"For the Lord is the Spirit, and wherever the Spirit of the Lord is, there is freedom. So all of us who have had that veil removed can see and reflect the glory of the Lord. And **the Lord - who is the Spirit** - makes us more and more like him as we are changed into his glorious image"* (2 Corinthians 3:17-18).

True born-again Christians do not worship three gods. The Jewish prayer in the Bible, called the Shema, speaks of only one true God. *"Listen, O Israel! The LORD is our God, the LORD alone"* (Deuteronomy 6:4).

Jesus answers a scribe who is asking Him what the greatest commandment was by quoting the Shema: *"Jesus replied, 'The most important commandment is this: "Listen, O Israel! The LORD our God is the one and only LORD'"* (Mark 12:29).

God being greater than everything He created and sovereign over it all can certainly exist as three persons in one supreme God. Why would He do that?

1) He came to earth in human form (Jesus Christ) for the express purpose of providing the only means of salvation for mankind. A complete sacrificial payment for all sin.

2) He then indwells everyone (Holy Spirit) who accepts and trusts His payment as a guarantee of His gift of eternal life and assurance of resurrection. The apostle Paul, speaking to Gentiles, told them, just like the Jews, they also could be saved by a Jewish Messiah. *And now you Gentiles have also heard the truth, the Good News that God saves you. And when you believed in Christ, he identified you as his own by giving you the Holy Spirit, whom he promised long ago. The Spirit is God's guarantee that he will give us the inheritance he promised and that he has purchased us to be his own people. He did this so we would praise and glorify him* (Ephesians 1:13-14).

3) Every born-again believer has God's power, His Holy Spirit, inside them. A power unlike any other enabling them to overcome sin, and guide and direct them every day in their lives. *"Now all glory to God, who is able, through his mighty power at work within us, to accomplish infinitely more than we might ask or think"* (Ephesians 3:20).

4) The Lord God is the only true God. *"I am the First and the Last; there is no other God"* (Isaiah 44:6).

God said it, I believe it, it's settled. Some may see this expression as narrow closed-mindedness. A lot more is going on here. This slogan expresses a complete confidence in the authority of the Bible. It's hard to criticize someone for firmly believing the Bible contains God's instructions to the human race.[34] It's not man's opinion or idea, it's God's.

We may not be able to explain it, but there clearly is three distinct personalities in one God. In God's world, one plus one plus one does equal one … three in one.

---

[34] (https://www.dictionaryofchristianese.com/god-said-it-i-believe-it-that-settles-it/)

Chapter 20: Are We Miserable to the Max

Nobody wants to be miserable. Certainly not stay miserable. Dictionary.com defines miserable as "wretchedly unhappy, uneasy, or uncomfortable."

Born-again Christians have more to be happy about than anyone else. They are assured of an eternal home in a perfect heaven. A place without pain, tears, sorrow, suffering, jealousy, anger, and the list goes on and on. An assurance repeated in God's Word, the Bible:

"I give them eternal life, and they will never perish. No one can snatch them away from me, John 10:28; *I tell you the truth, anyone who believes has eternal life"* (John 6:47); *"I have written this to you who believe in the name of the Son of God, so that you may know you have eternal life"* (1 John 5:13). Just a few of the many "God assurances" promised to His children.

But here's the kicker: Every Christian can be the most miserable person in the world. Certainly, seems like a contradiction to the first sentence in the second paragraph.

We are promised a resurrection from the grave after we die. A guarantee that is nullified if Jesus did not rise from the dead. The Apostle Paul writes, *"And if Christ has not been raised, then your faith is useless, and you are still guilty of your sins. In that case, all who have died believing in Christ are lost! And if our hope in Christ is only for this life, we are more to be pitied than anyone in the world"* (1 Corinthians 15:17-19).

So how can we be certain Jesus rose from the grave? The introduction of this book gave some insights. First, the Bible states Jesus was seen by more than 500 of his followers in 1 Corinthians 15:4-7. Another proof is the martyred death of his disciples. Why would they die for a dead Savior and a false gospel message?

But one of the most powerful confirmations is the prophesies of His resurrection. How would a dead Jesus deliver a fatal crushing blow to Satan as prophesied in Genesis 3:15 if He remained in a tomb? If any god could not resurrect themself from a grave, how could they resurrect human beings? No other god has accomplished their own resurrection.

King David declares, *"No wonder my heart is glad, and I rejoice. My body rests in safety. For you will not leave my soul among the dead or allow your Holy One to rot in the grave."* Who is

God's Holy One? Not David, but none other than Jesus. How in the world would David have known both Jesus and he would not remain dead? His excitement did not come from a false hope or assumption. It had to come from divine revelation. And God had not yet come to earth as Jesus Christ.

How would we as God's children be the most miserable people alive or dead? If we are worshiping a dead god and savior, we're missing out on the "fun" and "excitement" we could be having as unbelievers? We've devoted our lives to church attendance, Bible studies, devotions, prayer, and service to what end?

We have an exciting life with a purpose greater than any other. Not a miserable life ending in a miserable grave and separated from the one true God in hell, a place of eternal torment … miserable to the max.

Chapter 21: Details, Details, Details

How do we know a prediction or prophecy is true and from God? There's an abundant supply of prophets, seers, fortune tellers, and palm readers predicting future events. If their prediction is accurate, can we assume they are a reliable and legitimate forth-teller? No way!

For example, there's been a plethora of predictors of the end of the world. "Among the most prolific modern predictors of end times, Harold Camping has publicly predicted the end of the world as many as 12 times based on his interpretations of biblical numerology. In 1992, he published a book, ominously titled *1994*, which predicted the end of the world sometime around that year. Perhaps his most high-profile predication was for May 21, 2011, a date that he calculated to be exactly 7,000 years after the Biblical flood. When that date passed without incident, he declared his math to be off and pushed back the end of the world to October 21, 2011."[35]

Jeremiah Johnson, a 33-year old self-described prophet, predicted Donald Trump would be re-elected in 2020. Psychic Jeane Dixon's greatest claim to fame was announcing John F. Kennedy would be assassinated. She "claims to be a prophet of God, one who is doing 'the Lord's work.'" In fact, she has gone so far as to say that "the same spirit that worked through Isaiah and John the Baptist also works through me.'"[36] A mathematician at Temple University, John Allen Paulos, coined the phrase "the Jeane Dixon effect" referring to the promotion of her few correct predictions while ignoring her many erroneous ones.[37] Ever hear of even a few of her numerous false predictions? Her fallacies include: what would start WWII, Walter Reuther running for president, the second child of a Canadian Prime Minister being a girl (it was a boy).[38]

What happened to false prophets in Bible days? They ceased to exist. They were killed, probably stoned to death. "*But any prophet who falsely claims to speak in my name or who speaks in the name of another god must die*" (Deuteronomy 18:20).

---

[35] (https://www.britannica.com/list/10-failed-doomsday-predictions)
[36] https://www.equip.org/articles/jeane-dixon-and-prophecy/
[37] (http://www.fact-index.com › jeane_dixon)
[38] (https://en.wikipedia.org/wiki/Jeane_Dixon)

Woah! It sure would reduce the number of fortune tellers, seers and prophets today if one erroneous forecast led to their death.

Biblical prophecies add an unparalleled validity to the Bible being God's Word, not man's. To date, they've all been accurate and fulfilled in detail.

But what really adds to its authenticity and reliability is the details in biblical prophecies.

If I were to predict that a car accident would happen exactly a month from today in the city I live in, I would hear a bunch of "so what's." Probably no one would listen to any other prophecy I would make. But, if I said a red 1970 VW bug would collide with a classic yellow 1936 Ford pickup at the intersection of 46th Street and 43rd Avenue in Vero Beach, Florida at 2:18 a.m. three weeks from today, I'd get a lot of followers if it happened exactly as I detailed it. There would still be some skeptics wondering how in the world I knew what would happen. Was I driving the car and a friend the truck?

Look at the prophecies about Tyre, (chapter 21). Investigate the many detailed Messianic prophecies of genealogy (chapter 23), His coming (chapter 15), birthplace (chapter 16), appearance, rejection, torture (chapter 17), death (Chapter 24), resurrection (chapter 19), and purpose for coming (chapters 32,33,36, and 38).

The Bible is full of details on top of details.

HISTORICAL FACTS

Chapter 22: Against All Odds

Ever play the odds? We definitely want the odds in our favor. When they're not, it's really risky. Who wants odds like the lottery or PCH (Publishers Clearing House)?

One of the most outstanding "against-all-odds" biblical historical prophecies was about the city of Tyre in Israel. The listing includes:

1. Many nations would come against Tyre. (Ezekial 26:3)
2. The walls of Tyre would be broken down. (Ezekial 26:4)
3. Dust would be scraped from Tyre. She would be left like a bare rock. (Ezekial 26:4)
4. Tyre would be a place for the spreading of nets. (Ezekial 26:5)
5. Nebuchadnezzar, king of Babylon, would bring a siege against Tyre. (Ezekial 26:8)
6. Nebuchadnezzar would plunder the city. (Ezek. 26:9-12)
7. The stones, timber and soil of Tyre would be cast into the sea. (Ezekial 26:12)
8. The city would never be rebuilt (Ezekial 26:14)

Historical facts about Tyre:

1. It was considered the greatest sea empire in ancient history- the center of world commerce. No surprise predicting many would try to conquer this great city. Odds are stacked in the gambler's favor.

2. After a siege of 13 years (573 B.C.), Nebuchadnezzar conquered Tyre (an amazing fulfillment of prophecies #5 and #6) Wow, thirteen years!

3. The inhabitants of Tyre fled to a rocky island half a mile offshore. The walls on the landward side of the island were 150 feet high. "The channel between Tyre and the mainland was over twenty feet deep, and frequently lashed by violent south-west winds. (Prophecy #8 seems impossible)

4. The Tyrians refused to surrender to Alexander the Great. He then constructed a causeway connecting the island to the mainland. This was one of the most difficult and astounding marine engineering tasks of that era. The stones and tree limbs from the ruins of ancient Tyre were thrown into the water. Sand was placed on top of them. (the improbable fulfillment of prophesies #3 and #7 were fulfilled; Alexander's army now conquered Tyre, #2)

5. The land was eventually resettled by new peoples. To this day, the causeway still remains. The place where Tyre originally stood is now where fishermen dry their nets, just as Ezekiel foretold. (#3, #4, and #8 were completely fulfilled)[39]

If we were into betting, what do we think the odds of all of these prophecies coming true would be? A conservative one thousand to one? No, more like lotteries or PHC's millions to one.

Do you see the vital importance of details, details, details when it comes to making valid prophecies, predictions, or fortune telling? God sure gives them.

---

[39] (https://beliefmap.org/prophecy-fulfilled/tyre)

Chapter 23: God's Starting Overs

Quite a few times the Lord God was so angered at the sinfulness of mankind, He wanted to wipe them out and start over. The most notable one in the Bible was the flood.

"Make the boat 450 feet long, 75 feet wide, and 45 feet high" (Genesis 6:15), were God's instructions to Noah. Not just a little boat to save Noah and his family. A monster of a boat. The length would be four and a half football-fields long, almost a football field in width, and over four stories high.

Here's Noah, scratching his head and asking, "What's an ark? What's a flood? Why me?" God told Noah He was fed up with the wickedness of mankind. *"The LORD observed the extent of human wickedness on the earth, and he saw that everything they thought or imagined was consistently and totally evil"* (Genesis 6:5).

It's not certain how long it took Noah to build the ark? The life-size ark at Ark Encounter in Williamstown, Kentucky, took a little over six years to build from contract to completion. They state, "The likely view is that it took a maximum of 75 years to build Noah's Ark. When God told Noah to build the Ark, he said that it would be for Noah, his wife, their three sons, and their sons' wives (Genesis 6:18). It seems God did not tell Noah about the upcoming flood until Noah's sons were already grown up and married. Assuming a minimum of 25 years from Noah's 500th year to allow for his sons to be born, mature, and marry, then Noah would have had a maximum of 75 years to build the ark." Remember, Noah didn't have modern tools.[40]

Can we imagine the ridicule Noah received during the many years he was building this mammoth monstrosity? Genesis 2:5-6 seems to indicate no rain had ever occurred before the flood. *"...For the LORD God had not yet sent rain to water the earth, and there were no people to cultivate the soil. Instead, springs came up from the ground and watered all the land."* When Noah was

---

[40] (https://arkencounter.com/blog/2019/03/28/noahs-ark-vs-ark-encounter-whats-the-difference/)

asked why he was building this massive boat, and he replied that God was going to flood the earth with water, the laughter was probably heard for miles.

Not much different from the response of skeptics today asking how in the world could the entire earth be completely covered with water, even if it did rain for forty days and forty nights (Genesis 7:17; 8:6). Verse 11 in Genesis 7 reads, "*all the underground waters erupted from the earth, and the rain fell in mighty torrents from the sky.*"

An article from *https://www.icr.org/article/springs-ocean* says, "Although scientists have examined only a small portion of ocean floor, seafloor springs appear to be common along the 40,000-mile Mid-Oceanic Ridge system. Dr. John M. Edmond of M.I.T. suggests that water circulation through oceanic springs is a major geologic process; he estimates that 40 cubic miles of water flow out of earth's oceanic springs each year."

God asked Job, "*Have you explored the springs from which the seas come? Have you explored their depths?*" (Job 38:16) There's no way Job had done this. Even today so little has been discovered of what lies at the bottom of the ocean under the extreme pressure of boatloads of water.

A world-wide flood covering everything by torrents of water from the sky and ocean depths would account for the deposits of organic material, formation of mountains and canyons like the Grand Canyon and others, in a comparatively short period of time instead of millions of years.

Ancient civilizations have supported evidence of a great flood. "New research recently published in the *Science* magazine by a group of mostly Chinese researchers led by Qinglong Wu reports geological evidence for an event they propose may be behind China's story of a great flood."[41] Dr. Robert Ballard, an acclaimed underwater archaeologist, has found evidence that may support a worldwide flood about the time of Noah.[42]

Thank God for His promise to never destroy mankind again with a flood. A promise sealed by rainbows. "*Yes, I am confirming my covenant with you. Never again will floodwaters kill all living creatures; never again will a flood destroy the earth. Then God said, I am giving you a sign of my covenant with you and with all living creatures, for all generations to come. I have placed my rainbow in the clouds. It is the sign of my covenant with you and with all the earth*" (Genesis 9:11-13). Rainbows are beautiful. Stunning reminders of God's unending love, mercy, and grace for all mankind. Mankind who daily ignore, disrespect, disobey, and curse Him.

But Scripture also tells us the end of all mankind on earth will come again at the end of the Great Tribulation and the Battle of Armageddon. Thank God as born-again believers we need not fear this for we will already be in God's presence. We will see Him start over again with a new heaven and a new earth, wherein dwells righteousness. "*Looking forward to the day of God and hurrying it along. On that day, he will set the heavens on fire, and the elements will melt away in the flames. But we are looking forward to the new heavens and new earth he has promised, a world filled with God's righteousness*" (2 Peter 3:12-13).

---

[41] "https://www.scientificamerican.com/article/ancient-chinese-megaflood-may-be-fact-not-fiction/"

[42] (https://abcnews.go.com/Technology/evidence-suggests-biblical-great-flood-noahs-time-happened/story?id=17884533)

Reminds me of the song, "What a day that will be when my Jesus I shall see, when I look upon His face, the one who saved me by His grace; when He takes me by the hand and leads me through the Promised Land, what a day glorious day that will be." What a "start over!"

As God's children we need to warn an ungodly world of God's final start over plan. Many may scoff and site the fact we are centuries removed from any supposed flood and no Savior has come as the Bible promises. 2 Peter 3:9 gives this insight. *"The Lord isn't really being slow about his promise, as some people think. No, he is being patient for your sake. He does not want anyone to be destroyed, but wants everyone to repent."*

The signs are evident. Luke 17:26-27 states, *"When the Son of Man returns, it will be like it was in Noah's day. In those days, the people enjoyed banquets and parties and weddings right up to the time Noah entered his boat and the flood came and destroyed them all."* Second Timothy 3:1-5 (KJV) gets more descriptive, *"This know also, that in the last days perilous times shall come. For men shall be lovers of their own selves covetous, boasters, proud, blasphemers, disobedient to parents, unthankful, unholy, without natural affection, trucebreakers, false accusers, incontinent, fierce, despisers of those that are good, traitors, heady, high-minded, lovers of pleasures more than lovers of God;* ***H****aving a form of godliness, but denying the power thereof: from such turn away."*

Some may say, there's always been these kinds of people on the earth. Not like we see today. Just single out "disobedient to parents" and "without natural affection" in the context of "proud."

Being a parent, and a junior high and high school teacher, I can affirm it's a whole different ballgame today, compared to when I was a kid over sixty years ago. I've taught in Christian, public, rural, and inner-city schools. The lack of respect for authority runs rampant in our society and is certainly not on a downward trend.

Stand in a store check-out line and watch kids pitch tantrums over what they want, until their frustrated and embarrassed parents submit to their demands. Regardless of your beliefs about gay pride, it's celebrated and proclaimed in every way possible. To believe these examples are not blatantly different, nor more pronounced than in the past, requires a pair of blinders shrouding the eyes.

It's getting close to God's final "Starting-over time."

Chapter 24: Weird Genealogy

Ever research your genealogy? It can be interesting to find out who your ancestors were. Your efforts can be rewarded with excitement or embarrassment. You would hope for some relatives noted for their godly character and beneficial accomplishments for their culture. Wouldn't the most notable people in history have outstanding genealogies?

The most notable personality in the past is Jesus. Regardless of your belief in the Bible, God, or Jesus, His life on earth was unparalleled by any other. Who else has performed the miracles He did? Who else, of their own power, has come back from the dead?

Jesus made an exclusive statement of being the one and only way to heaven for every human being: *"I am the way, the truth, and the life. No one can come to the Father except through me."* Not one of many ways, take your pick. The belief of all people going to heaven, just going different ways, sounds great and very attractive. But the Bible declares there's only one way and one truth on how anyone gets to heaven. Not everyone is going to heaven.

God declares He was and is the only true God. God who came to earth as Jesus Christ. Remember, Jesus Christ asserts, *"If you had known me, you would have known my Father also. From now on you do know him and have seen him. Philip said to him, 'Lord, show us the Father, and it is enough for us.' Jesus said, 'Have I been with you so long, and you still do not know me, Philip? Whoever has seen me has seen the Father. How can you say, 'Show us the Father?'"* (John 14:7-9) Why is one of Jesus' many titles "the **Lord** Jesus Christ?"

Look at His genealogy chart recorded in Mathew 1:1-17 and Luke 3:23-38:

Most people who know anything about the Bible recognize the outstanding names of Adam, Noah, Abraham, King David, and King Solomon. Their well-known accomplishments include:

- Adam being the first human being on earth,
- Noah building a colossal ark, even though ridiculed by people who did not know what rain was;

- Abraham demonstrating a willingness to kill his own son, as God commanded.
- David, a giant slayer, and man after God's own heart, and
- Solomon who was blessed with more wisdom from God than probably anyone else.

But there's a flip side to each of these Bible celebrities:
- Adam blatantly disobeyed God's command not to eat the fruit from only one tree in a garden of trees. He also passed the buck blaming God for making Eve;
- Noah got drunk and naked after saving his family and all the animals
- David had sex with Uriah's wife, and had him murdered trying to cover His sin
- Solomon not only disobeyed God by marrying foreign pagan women but ended up worshipping their false gods.

So why put these sinners in the lineage of Jesus, the Messiah and Savior of the world? Why not stick with ones like Joseph who endured all kinds of persecution, eventually saving a nation and his family, including the brothers who hated him and tried to kill him. How about Job who God said: *"Have you noticed my servant Job? He is the finest man in all the earth. He is blameless, a man of complete integrity. He fears God and stays away from evil"* (Job 1:8). Who after losing his seven children, all his livestock and servants, and was covered from head to toe with boils, exclaimed, *"The LORD gave me what I had, and the LORD has taken it away. Praise the name of the LORD!"* (Job 1:21b).

It doesn't end with these. Jesus' family tree includes:
- Rahab, a prostitute,
- Nasty kings like Ahaz who burned his own son as a sacrifice to other gods,

Come on! The omnipotent (all powerful) and omniscient (all wise) God of the universe, who created everything and could do anything anyway He wants, certainly could pick and choose the best representatives of Godliness who would ever live. No, instead, He chose men and women just like you and me, sinners.

Much of His genealogy was prophesied in Genesis, chapters 22, 26, 28, 49 and Isaiah 11.

In man's logic this sounds weird. Not just weird, unthinkable. Another evidence of God's amazing grace consistently poured out on all His creation, especially mankind.

Chapter 25: To Die For

Ever want something so bad you would do anything to get it? "To die for" is a phrase often used to describe this kind of desire. Although, if it came right down to it, the one's saying this, probably would not literally die to obtain it.

What's worth dying for? Someone or something you love more than anything else, even your own life. Look at how many have willingly died defending their country, a cause, or their religious beliefs.

Such was the case with Jesus' closest disciples being martyred, refusing to deny their beliefs and the message they proclaimed.

1. James the son of Zebedee was executed by Herod.
2. Paul was beheaded in Rome about 66 AD.
3. Peter was crucified upside down at his request, since he felt he was not worthy to die in the same manner as his Lord Jesus Christ.
4. Andrew is said to have been crucified.
5. Thomas according to tradition died when pierced with the spears of four soldiers in India.
6. Philip converted the wife of a Roman proconsul. In retaliation, the proconsul had Philip arrested and cruelly put to death.
7. Some reports say Matthew was stabbed to death in Ethiopia.
8. There are various accounts of how Bartholomew met his death as a martyr for the gospel.
9. The Jewish historian Josephus reports James the son of Alpheus being stoned and then clubbed to death.
10. Simon the Zealot was killed after refusing to sacrifice to the sun god.

11. Matthais, the apostle chosen to replace Judas, died by burning.

John is the only one generally thought to have died a natural death from old age. He was exiled to the island of Patmos where he wrote Revelation. An early Latin tradition has him escaping unhurt after being cast into boiling oil in Rome. A good reference book is *Foxes Book of Martyrs*.

Why would all these disciples who had spent almost three years, twenty-four/seven, with Jesus, suffer violent deaths for a false message and a man who wasn't who He said He was, God in the flesh, the Savior of mankind?

Many accounts tell of Christians giving their lives for the sake of the gospel:

Jim Elliot and four other missionaries were murdered by Auca Indians.

William Tyndale was strangled to death and burned at the stake.

Cyrus, Hazine and Yaron, converts from Islam to Christianity were martyred by their own friends and families. (https://htp.org/martyred-for-christ)

Listen to this account entitled "The Unashamed." In 1980 a young man from Rwanda was forced by his tribe to either renounce Christ or face certain death. He refused to renounce Christ, and he was killed on the spot. This was found in his Bible after he was martyred:

"I am part of the fellowship of the unashamed, the die has been cast, I have stepped over the line, the decision has been made - I am a disciple of Jesus Christ. I won't look back, let up, slow down, back away, or be still. My past is redeemed, my present makes sense, my future is secure. I'm finished and done with low living, sight walking, smooth knees, colorless dreams, tamed vision, worldly talking, cheap giving and dwarfed goals. My face is set, my gait is fast, my goal is heaven, my road is narrow, my way is rough, my companions are few, my guide is reliable, my mission is clear. I won't give up, shut up, let up until I've stayed up, stored up, prayed up for the cause of Jesus Christ. I must go till He comes, give till I drop, preach till everyone knows, work till He stops me and when He comes for His own, He will have no trouble recognizing me because my banner will have been clear … the fellowship of the unashamed."[43] What a testimony!

'*For I am not ashamed of this Good News about Christ. It is the power of God at work, saving everyone who believes - the Jew first and also the Gentile*" (Romans 1:16). No greater cause to die for!

The Bible says the greatest thing we could ever do to show love for someone is to die for them. "*There is no greater love than to lay down one's life for one's friends*" (John 15:13).

The greatest love ever shown was God coming to earth as Jesus Christ and culminating his life and ministry by dying on a cross to pay for all the sins of all mankind. "*But God showed his great love for us by sending Christ to die for us while we were still sinners*" (Romans 5:8). Not just dying for the ones He knew would accept Him as their only Savior, He died for the ones He knew would hate, despise, and reject Him. The very ones who tortured, mocked, spit on Him, and put Him to death.

No one will ever go to hell because they're a sinner. All sin for everyone there ever has been or ever will be is paid for. Writing to born-again believers, John records God's words in 1 John

---

[43] (https://www.gospeltruth.net/unashamed.htm)

2:2, "*He himself is the sacrifice that atones for our sins - and not only our sins but the sins of* **all** *the world.*)

The most important reason for God coming to earth as Jesus Christ was to die. Not only was His death prophesied thousands of years before His coming, but specific detail is also prophesied about the events leading up to His death and following His death.

Even Genesis 3:15 prophesied His death when you compare it with other Scriptures explaining how His death would "crush Satan's head." One of the greatest clear prophetical passages of Jesus' death and His greatest purpose for coming to earth is Isaiah 53:5-6. "*But he was pierced for our rebellion, crushed for our sins. He was beaten so we could be whole. He was whipped so we could be healed. All of us, like sheep, have strayed away. We have left God's paths to follow our own. Yet the* LORD *laid on him the sins of us all.*"

"Oh, how He loves you and me; Oh, how He loves you and me. He gave His life, what more could He do? Oh, how He loves you. Oh, how He loves me. Oh, how He loves you and me!"

The Lord Jesus Christ's message to everyone is "I came **to die for** you!"

FAIRY TALES or MIRACLES

Chapter 26: Bible Ghosts

Are there ghosts in the Bible? Skeptics say the Bible is unreliable because it mentions: the Hittite nation (Deuteronomy 7:1), cities like Nineveh (Jonah 1:1, 2), and Sodom (Genesis 19:1). They say there is no evidence of the existence of any of these. Some critics also say there's no evidence Kings Belshazzar (Daniel 5:1) and Sargon (Isaiah 20:1) ever existed. I'm sure the list goes on.

A Smithsonian magazine has an article (September 22, 2021) entitled "Ancient City's Destruction by Exploding Space Rock May Have Inspired Biblical Story of Sodom." It says, "Around 1650 B.C.E., the Bronze Age city of Tall el-Hammam was wiped out by a blast 1,000 times more powerful than the atomic bomb used at Hiroshima. Tell el-Hammam (also Tall al-Hammam) is an archaeological site in Jordan, in the eastern part of the lower Jordan Valley close to the mouth of the Jordan River." Some believe this city was the same as Sodom, others don't.

If archaeological evidence exists of a city being annihilated by an exploding comet or meteor, couldn't it have also happened to Sodom and Gomorrah?

Christianity Today magazine has an article titled "Sodom Destroyed by Meteor, Scientists Say. Biblical Archaeologists Not Convinced". It says few archaeologists believe Tall-el-Hamman was the Biblical Sodom.[44]

We come to a common scenario with Biblical events, especially supernatural ones. Some try to validate these events with scientific evidence. And if they can't, they not only ridicule the ones believing these events occurred but refuse to believe the Bible period. Others may pick and choose the parts of the Bible agreeing with their beliefs. No wonder we have so many religions believing so many different things.

The realm of the supernatural, by its own name, can preclude natural explanation or verification.

---

[44] *https://www.christianitytoday.com/news/2021/ september/sodom-meteor-biblical-archaeology-tall-el-hammam-airburst.html*

Many Biblical events defy scientific and logical explanation. There is much debate over supposed archaeological and scientific validation of some of these events. Does that mean they did not happen?

A lot of skepticism of supernatural Biblical events originate from people who do not believe in a one and only true God, or do not accept the Bible as the inherent word of God.

"All Scripture is inspired by God" (2 Timothy 3:16a) (some versions say "God breathed"). *"Above all, you must realize that no prophecy in Scripture ever came from the prophet's own understanding, or from human initiative. No, those prophets were moved by the Holy Spirit, and they spoke from God* (2 Peter 1:20-21).

A saying I remember from my college days said, "Don't throw the baby out with the bathwater." This book has presented numerous facts substantiated by scientific, historical, and prophetical accuracy and factual evidence. Are those going to be discounted based on some unexplainable Biblical accounts? How powerful is your god? The power of the God of the Bible is unmeasurable and incomparable with any other power or god.

Now all glory to God, who is able, through his mighty power at work within us, to accomplish infinitely more than we might ask or think (Ephesians 3:20).

Don't let a few "Bible ghosts" scare you to death. Especially a death without hope, eternally separated from the God who loves you more than anyone else. Read John 3:16-18 again.

Chapter 27: A HUGE Gulp

What's the hugest gulp you've ever taken? Was it in a contest? Was it at 7-Eleven? Often, it's the one who can drink the most beer the fastest. Ultimately the biggest gulper usually throws up along with other contestants.

The BIGGEST Gulp should remind us of the Bible story of Jonah and the big fish. Why does a fish swallow anything? It must be hungry and looking for food. Even the fearsome shark is on a quest for something to eat, not just a menacing creature on a mission to rip apart a human plaything.

One question the Jonah story evokes is could someone be swallowed by a whale or a big fish? Another one is if they could be swallowed, how could they survive, especially for three days?

There are two types of whales: baleen whales (fourteen species) and toothed whales (seventy-six species). Instead of teeth, Baleen whales have flexible hair-like plates to filter small organisms like plankton, algae, fish, and krill. Whales with teeth usually use them to capture their prey, not chew them up. They just swallow them.

Open wide and say "Ah"

How big is a whale's mouth? "The largest mouth in the world belongs to the bowhead whale and can measure 5 meters (16 feet) long, 4 meters (12 feet) high, and 2.5 meters (8 feet) wide."[45] Now that's huge! Two cars on top of each other could easily drive through its mouth. This whale is probably not the Jonah whale, since it lives its entire lifetime in Arctic or subarctic waters.

Although a humpback whale's mouth can open to ten feet, its throat is roughly the size of a human fist and can

---

[45] (https://www.guinnessworldrecords.com/world-records/largest-mouth)

only stretch to about 15 inches in diameter to accommodate a bigger meal. It probably couldn't swallow a human being unless it was a really small one.

A blue whale's jaw can dislocate, and its accordion-like mouth can stretch up to four times its normal size. About one hundred people can fit in a blue whale's mouth, but its throat is really small at four to eight inches.

Is there a whale with a throat big enough to swallow a human? A sperm whale has a throat large enough to swallow giant squid. They could swallow a human.

Can you imagine what it would be like being in a fish belly? Pitch black dark, ripe with a stinky smell, and sticky, but there's more problems. What about the digestive juices in the stomach and the absence of oxygen?

Sperm whales have a four-chambered stomach. Listen to this account: "The first stomach is called the fore stomach or rumen. The rumen is where food is stored and partially broken down with bacteria. The tissue of the rumen does not create digestive juices. This means that the contents in this first compartment could hold a food item without breaking it down chemically. Some wonder if there is enough air to survive in a whale's stomach. In the rumen, there tends to be no oxygen, as the microbes within that organ cannot live with oxygen present. This is true for a healthy rumen, however, air can be present in the case of ruminal tympathy (bloating). This would have been the case for Jonah. Whales breathe air, and if its stomach is upset it would be coming up frequently for more air and possibly swallowing some in."[46] Plus, bloating would likely lead to throwing up what's causing it's upset stomach. One of these whales would have no problem swallowing Jonah. But a human being would probably not be on its menu.

Stories of people being swallowed by whales have existed for some time. One happened in February 1891. James Bartley was a whaler on a whaling ship near the Falkland Islands. The sperm whale they were hunting capsized the boat he was in. Four other sailors were rescued, but he went missing. The bloated whale surfaced two days later. When the sailors were skinning the inflated whale, they detected something inside its stomach. Upon cutting the whale open they found James, almost unconscious, but alive! He died 18 years later. His gravestone in Gloucester, England reads: "James Bartley - a modern Jonah."[47]

Now for the seemingly greatest question: How could Jonah stay alive in the belly of a whale for three days and three nights. Even Mr. Bartley was only in a whale's belly for two days and was barely alive.

The God of Creation

Often, if a biblical event cannot be verified scientifically, it is discounted as a "fairy tale." This is especially true when the event seems miraculous as in the case of a human surviving three days inside a whale's stomach. God is the God of miracles. He created whales and everything in the universe and with a word could create a whale in which a human could survive for days. The

---

[46] (https://bibleask.org/can-human-live-inside-whale-like-story-of-jonah/)
[47] (https://www.scienceabc.com/humans/can-a-whale-swallow-you-whole.html)

Bible account specifically says, "*Now the* LORD *had arranged for a great fish to swallow Jonah. And Jonah was inside the fish for three days and three nights"* (Jonah 1:17).

The God of Life

If Jonah did not survive alive inside the whale for three days, God, who breathed life into the first human beings, could have brought Jonah back to life. He did it with a mummy wrapped Lazarus and Jarius' daughter.

He performed the greatest resurrection in history in coming back from the dead himself. Isn't it an interesting fact, both Jonah and Jesus Christ were "buried" for three days?

Jesus prophesied His own death, burial, and triumphant resurrection: *But Jesus replied, "Only an evil, adulterous generation would demand miraculous sign; but the only sign I will give them is the sign of the prophet Jonah. For as Jonah was in the belly of the great fish for three days and three nights, so will the Son of Man be in the heart of the earth for three days and three nights"* (Matthew 12:39-40). We have the completed Word of God and the indwelling tremendous power of God's Holy Spirit right inside of us. There is not the need for miracles and signs as there was in Jesus' days on earth and those who lived in Old Testament times. Not to say He does not perform miracles today. The need is not as great, especially for *an evil and adulterous generation.* Without a gospel message as a priority and emphasis, miracles may extend life here on earth, provide healing and blessings, but still leave a recipient destined to die with a Christless eternity in hell.

The born-again believer's assurance of resurrection after death relies solely on our Savior's coming back from the dead. As Paul proclaims about our resurrection when Jesus returns for us:

"*and he was shown to be the Son of God when he was raised from the dead by the power of the Holy Spirit. He is Jesus Christ our Lord"* (Romans 1:4).

"*Since we have been united with him in his death, we will also be raised to life as he was"* (Romans 6:5).

"*I want to know Christ and experience the mighty power that raised him from the dead. I want to suffer with him, sharing in his death, so that one way or another I will experience the resurrection from the dead!"* (Philippians 3:10-11)

Without Jesus Christ's resurrection, we are the epitome of foolishness: "*For if there is no resurrection of the dead, then Christ has not been raised either. And if Christ has not been raised, then all our preaching is useless, and your faith is useless. And we apostles would all be lying about God-for we have said that God raised Christ from the grave. But that can't be true if there is no resurrection of the dead. And if there is no resurrection of the dead, then Christ has not been raised. And if Christ has not been raised, then your faith is useless and you are still guilty of your sins. In that case, all who have died believing in Christ are lost! And if our hope in Christ is only for this life, we are more to be pitied than anyone in the world"* (1 Corinthians 15:13-19). Praise God for the assurance and guarantee His resurrection proclaims and provides.

"The Lord God is our sun and shield, no good thing will He withhold from those who walk rightly" (Psalm 84:11). What's the opposite of this promise? If we don't obey God, He will keep some of the good things He wants to give us, just like He did with Jonah.

Sing with me: "Trust and obey, for there's no other way to be happy in Jesus, but to trust and obey."

The greatest lesson we can learn from Jonah's story is to obey God. If Jonah had not run away from where God told him to go (Nineveh) he wouldn't have been a HUGE gulp! Don't be like Jonah, just another HUGE gulp.

Chapter 28: Another "Mr. Ed"

Ever hear a horse talk? Remember the TV program entitled "Mr. Ed"? It featured a talking horse.

Then there's the film "The Horse Whisperer" starring Robert Redford. He had an uncanny way of communicating with horses. Some will quickly say, these are fictional characters or stories.

An initial question might be, "Can animals really talk?" Certainly Cesar Millan, the well-known dog whisperer would affirm a resounding, "You bet they can." Many animal lovers would attest to this, saying they've witnessed animals talking to each other and to them.

Our dog, Sheba, an Alaskan Malamute, doesn't talk often. But when she really wants something, you should hear her talk. She also listens well. We can't say *walk*, *go*, or even the letter "w" without her ears perked up and her getting all excited and getting our shoes. Most animals quickly learn words and commands like *sit, lay down, roll over, shake paw, good girl, good boy,* or *bad dog.*

I've had four Alaskan Malamutes. All of them would sit down without a command when food or a treat was brought. They would wait for an "okay" or head nod to begin eating. Something few dogs would do. In addition, they would sit back down when anyone took their food and wait for an "okay." Malamutes rarely bark or speak. But, like most dogs, they readily speak with tail wagging, sad eyes, bristled hair, a lap request, or a strategically placed paw.

A radio personality once gave a list of differences between a wife and a dog. The one I remember said: "The later you are getting home the more upset your wife is," whereas, "The later you are getting home the happier your dog is to see you."

Animals communicate with each other, and not just verbally. Look at this you tube video:[48] What a riot!

Research shows: "Animals communicate using signals, which can include visual; auditory, sound-based; chemical (involving pheromones), or tactile, touch-based, cues. Communication behaviors can help animals find mates, establish dominance, defend territory, coordinate group behavior, and care for young."[49]

A bizarre passage in the Old Testament takes place in Numbers 22-24 with Balaam and his talking donkey. When reading the context of this event, the donkey sees an angel with a sword blocking the path he is taking his master on. Balaam can't see the angel at first, so he beats his animal when he can't get it to move. The donkey asks, *"What have I done to you that deserves your beating me three times?"* (Numbers 22:28) Balaam doesn't seem to be surprised at his donkey talking. *"You have made me look like a fool!" Balaam shouted. "If I had a sword with me, I would kill you!"* (Verse 29) No doubt, an Old Testament example of "road rage." The conversation doesn't stop here. *"But I am the same donkey you have ridden all your life,"* the donkey answered. *"Have I ever done anything like this before?"* Balaam admitted, "No." (Verse 30)

I've heard a reference to people talking to themselves saying, it's okay to talk to yourself as long as you don't answer yourself. At least neither one of them started talking to themselves or answering themselves. Although I'll bet the donkey wanted to.

It's very important to notice two things in this unusual and humorous story. First of all, the Lord gave the donkey the ability to speak (Verse 28). Then in Verse 31, the Lord opened Balaam's eyes, and he saw the angel of the Lord standing in the roadway with a drawn sword in his hand.

Often God has to use drastic measures to get our attention.

Don't many animals possess keen senses much better than humans? Wouldn't you have something to say after being beat when all you're trying to do is help someone? In this case, save his master's life. The context says God was angry with Balaam because he did not obey His command not to go on this trip in the first place.

We need to back up in this story to understand what Balaam was doing against God's will. Balaam was on a mission after refusing repeated requests to curse the Israelites, a people God blessed ever since He created them. God specifically told Balaam not to go. He obeyed at first, even though it meant forfeiting a huge reward he could have retired with.

When he was approached a second time with an even bigger enticement, he wanted to see if God would change His mind. God allowed Balaam to go even though it was against His perfect will. We can relate. Often, we ask God for something, and repeatedly ask, not willing to accept

---

[48] (https://www.youtube.com/watch?v=drLzPZVox9Q)
[49] (https://www.khanacademy.org/science/ap-biology/ecology-ap/responses-to-the environment/a/animal-communication)

His initial answer. His answer can be "no", "wait", or the "yes" we often want to hear. Like Balaam, without a "yes", we may keep on asking, thinking our prayers haven't been answered.

Dr. David Jeremiah says there are four ways God answers our prayers: "no," "wait," "yes," or "you've got to be kidding me." I'm sure he's answered a lot of mine with the last option.

The God who created all the different races and languages of the "Babelian" people, because they were building a tower in an effort to reach heaven, could easily allow a donkey to speak "human."

The Babel event parallels many of today's religions purporting all types of human effort to get to heaven on their own merit. Even heaven was purged of angels and their leader who wanted to be God.

Psalm 14:3 states, "*But no, all have turned away; all have become corrupt. No one does good, not a single one!*" Romans 3:10 and 3:23 confirm this fact: "*As the Scriptures declare, No one is righteous - not even one.*" Likewise, Isaiah 53:6 records, "*All we like sheep have gone astray; We have turned, everyone, to his own way.*" Thank God the verse doesn't end there but reveals our only means of eternal life in heaven: "*And the LORD has laid on Him, (Jesus), the iniquity of us all.*"

If we don't listen to and obey God and His word, the Bible, He uses other means to get our attention, just like He did with Balaam. He used a "dumb" talking donkey. A donkey who was smarter than his master.

"A horse is a horse, of course, of course, and no one can talk to a horse, of course.

That is, of course, unless the horse is the famous Mister Ed. The show said Mister Ed shares his words of wisdom only with Wilbur, his hapless owner."[50]

Listen to and obey the God who created animals. Animals who sometimes are wiser than their owners.

[50] https://www.lyricsondemand.com/tvthemes/mredlyrics.html

Chapter 29: The Final Parting Ways

Technology affords a variety of means to "part ways" with someone. You can unfriend, unfollow, snooze, block, or delete them.

The Bible tells of the unique ways the Egyptians and Israelites parted company. It took ten plagues, worse than Covid, for Pharoah to cave. Can you visualize all your water turning to blood, every place you go or hide you find frogs, lice or gnats, flies, locusts, darkness, dead livestock, hail, and everyone covered with boils? Even with all those plagues, it took the death of every firstborn Egyptian child for them to finally part ways (Exodus chapters 7-11).

But this parting was only temporary. Soon after the Israelites left, the "can't-make-up-my-mind" Pharoah and his army are in hot pursuit of the escapees. Trapped at the Red Sea, the Israelites wished they were still slaves in Egypt. They blamed God and Moses for their seemingly imminent death.

Then with the stroke of a rod, God parted the Red Sea, and an estimated two to three million Israelites crossed the Red Sea. They didn't trudge across in mud, but on dry land (Exodus 14:21).

Some say there was a spelling error in this biblical account. Instead of the Red Sea, it was the Reed Sea or Sea of Reeds, a huge marsh. For sure, the Israelites could cross a marsh without a miracle from God. But what a miracle it would be for the entire Egyptian army to drown in a marsh.

Much controversy surrounds whether or not chariot wheels and other artifacts supporting the biblical account of the Egyptian army drowning in the Red Sea have been found.

Regardless of any scientific or archeological facts supporting this biblical event, the God who created everything in the universe, including the Red Sea, could certainly part it by the same words of creation. He spoke, it happened, repeatedly.

God wants everyone to go to heaven. *"This is good and pleases God our Savior, who wants everyone to be saved and to understand the truth"* (1 Timothy 2:3-4).

Chapter 30: "Whoa" Sun

What would we do without the sun? We would quickly die. It's our source of light and life. Some of the many benefits of the sun include:

1. Improves your sleep creating the hormone melatonin
2. Reduces stress by regulating melatonin
3. Maintains strong bones producing vitamin D in our bodies
4. Helps keep the weight off – seems to help by being outside for 30 minutes sometime between 8 a.m. and noon
5. Strengthens your immune system with vitamin D which can reduce the risk of illness, infections, some cancers, and mortality after surgery
6. Fights off depression improving your mood increasing serotonin levels

It can give you a longer life. "A study that followed 30,000 Swedish women revealed that those who spent more time in the sun lived six months to two years longer than those with less sun exposure."[51]

Sun facts are mind boggling:

- The Sun's core temperatures reach at least 27,000,000 °F. Its surface has an average temperature of 9,941°F.
- The Sun is 92,955,807 miles from the Earth.
- It is the largest and most massive object in our solar system. It contains approximately 99.86 percent of all the mass in our solar system.

---

[51] (https://selecthealth.org/blog/2020/07/7-health-benefits-of-sunlight)

- Being 100 Earths wide, it could theoretically fit all eight planets inside it nearly 600 times, or 1.3 million earths; Its diameter is 856,658 miles.
- There are much bigger stars. The biggest star we know of would almost reach Saturn if placed in the Solar System.
- Every second, the Sun provides energy equivalent to 10 billion nuclear bombs.
- Absence of sunlight would lower the Earth's temperature to about -148 °F (-100 °C) in a month, without a wind chill factor.
- A person weighing 165 pounds (75 kilograms) on planet Earth would weigh 4,466 pounds (2,025 kilograms) on the Sun's surface.
- its ultraviolet light has antiseptic properties and can sanitize water and tools.
- The outer atmosphere is hotter than the surface. Its chromosphere can reach 100,000°K. But that's nothing. The corona, which extends to a volume even larger than the Sun itself can reach 1 million °K.[52][53]

Wow! Some mind-boggling facts.

The Bible records some unusual sun events. Joshua 10:12-13 tells of God causing the sun to stand still during the day so the children of Israel could defeat the ungodly Amorites.

At the crucifixion of Jesus, the Bible records He died during the daytime and darkness covered the earth from noontime to 3 p.m. (Luke 23:44). A question posed to explain this event is, "Was this a solar eclipse?"

"The Gospels make clear Jesus was crucified during the Jewish festival of Passover … which is always celebrated during a full moon in spring. But a new moon is needed for a solar eclipse to occur, making it 'exactly the wrong phase of the moon.' Plus, the darkness that descended during the Crucifixion was too long to be a solar eclipse. The time from the beginning to end of a partial eclipse can run about three hours, but the darkness of a total solar eclipse only lasts a few minutes."[54]

Often people try to explain biblical events, especially miracles, as a scientific phenomenon. Many things in the Bible cannot be explained away by scientific facts. If one does not believe in one true supreme God, then they must explain things from a scientific approach to prove it was not a miracle.

I believe in a God of miracles. A God who spoke everything into being. In the Genesis 1 account of creation, each day of creation starts with the words *"Then God said,"* and ends with *"that is what happened."*

Jesus is called the Word and John 1:1-4 says by the Word everything was created: *In the beginning the Word already existed. The Word was with God, and the Word was God. He existed*

---

[52] https://www.universetoday.com/17982/10-interesting-facts-about-the-sun/

[53] https://www.surfertoday.com/environment/sun-50-amazing-facts-about-the-star-of-the-solar-system

[54] (https://www.sltrib.com/religion/global/2017/08/20/did-a-solar-eclipse-darken-the-skies-during-jesus-crucifixion)

in the beginning with God. God created everything through him, and nothing was created except through him. The Word gave life to everything that was created, and his life brought light to everyone.

The God who created everything by His word, could with the two words, "Whoa Sun," stop the sun in its track.

WHAT'S THE POINT

Chapter 31: To Be Morphed or Not Morphed

Change is difficult. Often, the older one gets the more resistant they are to change.

"If it's not broke, why fix it?" can seem the best way to go. After all, if what we like and the way we like it has always worked well, why ever consider changing?

Most change is making something or someone different, unlike the way it was before.

Change can be good or bad. But if there were no changes, mankind might still be prehistoric, living in caves and hunting dinosaurs.

Some things always change. We cannot stop time, weather from changing, prices escalating, feelings to cease, people multiplying, no seasons, nature evolving, and many other things from changing.

Look at technology. It's a world of continual alteration. Not only can people connect all over the world in seconds, but you can find a world of information for just about anything by pressing a few buttons. Who in the nineteenth century would have dreamed this would be possible?

We live in a world of change. Hasn't the Covid pandemic caused a world-wide change? Our world will never be the same again.

It has been said change can be hard at the beginning, messy in the middle, but gorgeous at the end. This is certainly true in nature. One striking example is that of the butterfly.

How many people like caterpillars? Some weird looking insects crawling and twisting in many shapes and colors. This insect can have more than four thousand muscles in their body, can increase in size by one thousand times in two to four weeks, has twelve eyes that can only perceive light and dark, and their only goal in life is to eat.

Then this unique creature builds an odd-shaped casket. One of the weirdest is made by bagworms, which is not a worm but a moth caterpillar. Its cocoon looks like a bag with pieces of twigs or leaves pasted all over it. Likewise, butterflies go through a chrysalis or pupa stage. The caterpillar's body dies and after a couple of weeks a new, beautiful body with wings appears.

Although a few butterflies can live from six to twelve months, the average life cycle of most are three to four weeks. With such a short lifespan, no wonder there are 17,000 to 165,000 (depending on what source is used) different species of butterflies.

All these changes occur within a few weeks and then the caterpillar and butterfly are gone. But in this brief lifespan, a butterfly has benefited mankind by pollinating fruits, vegetables, and flowers. Although bees and some insects are better pollinators, none are as beautiful as the butterfly.

The greatest and most beneficial change for all mankind came when God came to earth as Jesus, in a human form, and provided an eternal change no one else could accomplish. Isaiah 53:6 reads, "*All of us, like sheep, have strayed away. We have left God's paths to follow our own. Yet the LORD laid on him the sins of us all.*" Two verses in Romans 3:23 and 6:23 essentially say the same thing: "*For everyone has sinned; we all fall short of God's glorious standard; For the wages of sin is death, but the free gift of God is eternal life through Christ Jesus our Lord.*"

Accepting and trusting the complete payment Jesus Christ has made for all our sins gives us eternal life. *God saved you by his grace when you believed. And you can't take credit for this; it is a gift from God. Salvation is not a reward for the good things we have done, so none of us can boast about it* (Ephesians 2:8-9).

As if this change isn't enough, a new life here on earth is available to every born-again believer. This is what Jesus said His purpose was in addition to providing eternal life: "*My purpose is to give them a rich and satisfying life*" (John 10:10b). Not a perfect life, or one free of problems, but one with purpose and direction. A life with the power of God, the Holy Spirit, within us to face life's difficulties and show others what God is like. "*For we are God's masterpiece. He has created us anew in Christ Jesus, so we can do the good things he planned for us long ago*" (Ephesians 2:10).

Trusting Jesus for your eternal destiny is a change worth making. A change not only for life after death, but a better change right here and now.

There are many religious beliefs in the world. To change from one religious belief to another is often met with resistance, defiance, or anger. But I don't know of a more beautiful message or transformation than the one just described.

Metamorphosis … "A change of the form or nature of a thing or person into a completely different one, by natural or supernatural means."

The Bible says a person must repent to be saved. The Greek word for "repent," in the context of salvation, is "metanoia" meaning "a change of mind." One must abandon a belief that any human effort or goodness will merit eternal life in a perfect heaven. They must change their mind and accept and trust Christ's payment for all their sin, and nothing or no one else. "*He saved us, not because of the righteous things we had done, but because of his mercy. He washed away our sins, giving us a new birth and new life through the Holy Spirit*" (Titus 3:5).

"Jesus paid it all, all to Him I owe, sin had left a crimson stain, He washed it white as snow."

I've morphed, have you?

Chapter 32: Blessed Assurance

What's the only things we can be sure of? Death and taxes would be the response of many. There seems to be less and less things we can be absolutely certain of.

Even though I've accepted the complete payment Jesus Christ has made for all my sin and am trusting only Him and nothing or no one else to get me to heaven, I occasionally have had questions and doubts if I am truly saved. Especially when I continue to fail or disobey Him, even continuing to do the very thing I've just confessed to Him.

Now, when those doubts come, I remember a verse I've memorized, John 10:28. Jesus Himself promised, *"I give them eternal life, and they will; never perish. No one can snatch them away from me.* What great assurance this gives me."

There are three Greek words for our English word "never" in this verse. One word is "oume," which means "not at all, by no means, in no case." Another word is "eis," with the meaning "regardless of place or time." The last word is "aion" meaning "forever, eternally." (Strong's Concordance)

Put those three meanings in the verse and it reads, *I give them eternal life; and they shall not at all, by no means, in no way, regardless of place or time, forever or eternally perish, No one can snatch them away from me.* There's assurance magnified!

When those doubts come crashing in, and they will, bombard them with a "Greek" John 10:28. How blessed is the assurance given you and me by Jesus, our Savior.

Many clear verses in the Bible gives each born-again believer confidence in their salvation: Jesus said, *"I tell you the truth, anyone who believes has eternal life"* (John 6:47).

The NKJV begins this verse with "Most assuredly...". ESV states, "Truly, truly...". NIV emphasizes, 'Very truly...'. Get the point?

One of the most definitive assurance passages, to every believer, is found in Romans 8, verses 31-35 and 37-39, "*What shall we say about such wonderful things as these? If God is for us, who can ever be against us? Since he did not spare even his own Son but gave him up for us all, won't he also give us everything else? Who dares accuse us whom God has chosen for his own? No one—for God himself has given us right standing with himself. Who then will condemn us? No one—for Christ Jesus died for us and was raised to life for us, and he is sitting in the place of honor at God's right hand, pleading for us. Can anything ever separate us from Christ's love? Does it mean he no longer loves us if we have trouble or calamity, or are persecuted, or hungry, or destitute, or in danger, or threatened with death? No, despite all these things, overwhelming victory is ours through Christ, who loved us. And **I am convinced that nothing can ever separate us from God's love**. Neither death nor life, neither angels nor demons, neither our fears for today nor our worries about tomorrow—not even the powers of hell can separate us from God's love. No power in the sky above or in the earth below—indeed, nothing in all creation will ever be able to separate us from the love of God that is revealed in Christ Jesus our Lord.*" No exclusions left out.

Probably the most well-known verse in the Bible is John 3:16. "*For this is how God loved the world: He gave His one and only Son, so that everyone who believes in Him will not perish but have eternal life.*"

The words "eternal" and "everlasting" are defined as "lasting or existing forever; without end or beginning." Even the words "saved," and "salvation" carry the meanings: "keep safe or rescue" and "preservation or deliverance."

If "salvation" or "eternal life" is something you can lose, then it would be the opposite of their very definitions.

Heavenly Father, thank you so much for the assuring promises you give me in Your Word. Please remind me of them when my doubts come. Thank you, Jesus.

"Blessed assurance, Jesus is mine! Oh, what a foretaste of glory divine! Heir of salvation, purchase of God, Born of His Spirit, washed in His blood. This is my story, this is my song, praising my Savior all the day long; This is my story, this is my song, praising my Savior all the day long. Perfect submission, all is at rest, I in my Savior am happy and blest, Watching and waiting, looking above, Filled with His goodness, lost in His love."

What a reassuring song of assurance.

Chapter 33: Faith Without Works: One or the Other

Peter wrote about Paul's writings in the Bible saying, "*speaking of these things in all of his letters. Some of his comments are hard to understand, and those who are ignorant and unstable have twisted his letters to mean something quite different, just as they do with other parts of Scripture. And this will result in their destruction*" (2 Peter 3:16).

We must compare hard to understand and difficult Bible verses and passages with easily understood scriptures in their context. Otherwise, the interpretation of these difficult passages are often left to one's biased beliefs. Then, it's no surprise there are so many different religious beliefs based on the same Bible.

One of the most glaring examples of this is found in James 2:18-24. Martin Luther, who nailed his "95 Theses" to the door of a Catholic church in 1517, which led to his excommunication from the Catholic church, did not think the book of James should be in the Bible. He believed it contradicted the gospel message of salvation by grace through faith. It certainly seems to be its message:

"*But someone will say, 'You have faith, and I have works. Show me your faith without your works, and I will show you my faith by my works.' You believe that there is one God. You do well. Even the demons believe—and tremble! But do you want to know, O foolish man, that faith without works is dead? Was not Abraham our father justified by works when he offered Isaac his son on the altar? Do you see that faith was working together with his works, and by works faith was made perfect? And the Scripture was fulfilled which says, 'Abraham believed God, and it was accounted to him for righteousness.' And he was called the friend of God. You see then that a man is justified by works, and not by faith only.*"

These verses seem to clearly show faith alone cannot save a person. It gives Abraham as the perfect example of being justified by his faith and his work, a willingness to offer his son Isaac on an altar as his Lord commanded.

When this passage is compared with Romans 4:1-5 (NKJV), a clearer and better understanding is found:

"What then shall we say that Abraham our father has found according to the flesh? ***For if Abraham was justified by works, he has something to boast about, but not before God.*** *For what does the Scripture say? 'Abraham believed God, and it was accounted to him for righteousness.' Now to him who works, the wages are not counted as grace but as debt.* ***But to him who does not work but believes on Him who justifies the ungodly, his faith is accounted for righteousness,"***

We are "justified" by our works in man's eyes, not God's. The only way we have a clue if someone is truly born again is by how they live their lives according to Christian principles found in the Bible. But even this can be deceptive. In Matthew 7:22-23 (NIV) God says, "***Many*** *will say to Me on that day, 'Lord, Lord, did we not prophesy in your name and in your name drive out demons and, in your name, perform many miracles?' Then I will tell them plainly,* ***'I never knew you. Away from me, you evildoers!'"*** Why would God call prophecies, exorcism, and many miracles done in His name evil? Because they were done by people who have not placed their complete trust in God's payment for all their sins as their only means of salvation.

The context of a well-known biblical account of Paul and Silas in prison gives us more insight:

"One day as we were going down to the place of prayer, we met a slave girl who had a spirit that enabled her to tell the future. She earned a lot of money for her masters by telling fortunes. She followed Paul and the rest of us, shouting, 'These men are servants of the Most High God, and they have come to tell you how to be saved.' This went on day after day until Paul got so exasperated that he turned and said to the demon within her, 'I command you in the name of Jesus Christ to come out of her.' And instantly it left her. Her masters' hopes of wealth were now shattered, so they grabbed Paul and Silas and dragged them before the authorities at the market-place. The whole city is in an uproar because of these Jews!" they shouted to the city officials. 'They are teaching customs that are illegal for us Romans to practice.' A mob quickly formed against Paul and Silas, and the city officials ordered them stripped and beaten with wooden rods. They were severely beaten, and then they were thrown into prison. The jailer was ordered to make sure they didn't escape. So the jailer put them into the inner dungeon and clamped their feet in the stocks" (Acts 16:16-24).

You probably know the rest of the story and the miracles to come.

The means of salvation must be clearly separated from the service or work God wants a believer to do after their salvation. Any work or service we do for our Lord and Savior, Jesus Christ, is in no way any means of obtaining our salvation or keeping it.

Clear Bible verses declare: *"And if by grace, then it is no longer of works; otherwise, grace is no more grace. But if it is of works, it is no longer of grace; otherwise, work is no more work"*

(Romans 11:5-6 NKJV). This verse gives two alternatives for salvation, either grace or works. But, it makes it very clear, it's one or the other and cannot be any mixture of both.

"He saved us, not because of the righteous things we had done, but because of his mercy. He washed away our sins, giving us a new birth and new life through the Holy Spirit" (Titus 3:5).

Salvation, our eternal life in heaven, is solely by God's undeserved grace! Our service should be out of a heart of pure love and thankfulness for what the Lord Jesus Christ has done for us.

Should a true born-again believer serve and obey the Lord Jesus Christ? Absolutely, but not as any means of obtaining or keeping their salvation.

God commands every believer in Ephesians 2:10: *"For we are His workmanship, created in Christ Jesus for good works, which God has before ordained that we **should** walk in them"* (Ephesians 2:10 KJV). Note the word "should" not "must." This is true service, not salvation!

This verse is preceded by Ephesians 2:8,9, *"God saved you by his grace when you believed. And you can't take credit for this; it is a gift from God. Salvation is not a reward for the good things we have done, so none of us can boast about it."*

The Bible assures us that we are born into God's family the moment we accept His payment for all our sins and place our trust in Him alone as ours means of salvation. Just like when we are born into an earthly family, any good father and mother wants to care for us and expects our obedience. But disobedience does not expel us from our earthly family. It should, however, bring consequences in the form of punishment. God promises the same to each of his children.

The concept of "You reap what you sow" is God's promise: *"Don't be misled—you cannot mock the justice of God. You will always harvest what you plant"* (Galatians 6:7).

If a person's works has any part in their salvation, then how much do they have to do to be saved? If going to church has a part in salvation, how many times can a person miss and still go to heaven? If there's anything anyone must do in addition to accepting and placing their complete trust in Christ's payment for all their sin, there can be no assurance of their eternal life in heaven. Once you have it, you could lose it again and again.

Many religions provide a list of dos and don'ts required to get to heaven. But not a quantitative number is given for each requirement in order to gain or lose your salvation.

Is it works without faith, or faith without works for an eternal home in heaven? It's one or the other, not both. (Romans 11:5-6 NKJV).

111

Chapter 34: BIG Little Things: Distinguishing Blessings from Coincidence

Ever wonder whether the little "good things" in your life are God's blessings or just coincidences? Come on, good things happen to everyone at one time or another.

As a Christian, what we may call blessings, someone else merely names as coincidences. Doesn't God have a lot more important BIG things to take care of than the little everyday happenings in our lives? Those thoughts have crossed my mind.

My family never had much money or material possessions. I remember when my dad was going to Bible college. The four of us lived in a little one-room apartment. Mom and dad slept on a single bed. I was on a fold-up cot, and my younger brother snuggled on top of a storage trunk. No A/C in the humid, sweltering, St. Louis, Missouri summers. I named the state of our affairs "Misseri." A community refrigerator in the hallway wasn't a safe place to keep anything for any length of time. One bathroom was available to everyone in the apartment building.

My dad usually pastored small churches. He worked a second job just to make ends meet.

I was brought up being very thrifty. Always finding the best deals and being able to use coupons was and still is a top priority.

To this day, some seventy plus years later, one of the most difficult situations I face is having to purchase something without being able to shop around for the best price and hopefully having an unexpired coupon. I remember my youngest son at about five years of age asking me if I had a coupon for a new refrigerator when ours died.

Sometimes, household goods were stockpiled when I found a sale and had multiple coupons. Occasionally, I would get things free and sometimes get money back. My wife told me our dog would die before eating all the dog food. A bit of exaggeration.

Oh, the frustration when I must buy something without a sale or a coupon. Eighty to ninety percent of those times, the items "just happen" to be on sale where I go to purchase them. I would label a once-in-a-while occurrence like these as "coincidence." Those things happen occasionally to most people. But it happens to me most of the time and has throughout my life. It's not coincidences, it's God's intervention and care! Just like He promises, *"Take delight in the LORD, and he will give you your heart's desires."* The definition for "delight" comes in the next verse: *"Commit everything you do to the LORD. Trust him, and he will help you"* (Psalm 37:4-5).

"Look at the birds. They don't plant or harvest or store food in barns, for your heavenly Father feeds them. And aren't you far more valuable to him than they are? Can all your worries add a single moment to your life? And why worry about your clothing? Look at the lilies of the field and how they grow. They don't work or make their clothing, yet Solomon in all his glory was no dressed as beautifully as they are. And if God cares so wonderfully for wildflowers that are here today and thrown into the fire tomorrow, he will certainly care for you. Why do you have so little faith? So don't worry about these things, saying, What will we eat? What will we drink? What will we wear? These things dominate the thoughts of unbelievers, you're your heavenly Father already knows all your needs. Seek the Kingdom of God – above all else, and Live righteously, and he will give you everything you need. So, don't worry about tomorrow, for tomorrow will bring its own worries. Today's trouble is enough for today" (Matthew 6:26-34).

I'm not saying I always commit everything I do to the Lord. It's so amazing when I see those things occur repeatedly even when I've not asked Him.

More examples include:

1) One night I was in major pain from a back and neck injury. Having just returned from two out-of-town trips during the Christmas/New Year holidays we were well over budget and exhausted. I could barely move. Reluctantly I agreed to see a massage therapist, still contending we couldn't afford it. Of all places, the therapist was doing treatments in a side room at a restaurant. I thought it was strange and was worried we might be expected to order food. Without giving you all the details, it ended up costing us a total of fifteen dollars, including the massage (normally $40-$60) and two meals with drinks (Totaling around $30).

2) A recent 1600+ mile trip to get our new baby, Sheba (an Alaskan Malamute puppy) ended with all our expenses paid and an offer to dog sit any time we needed it. We've already repeatedly used the offer. We brought back three other puppies for a co-worker and two other parties.

3) Multiple times I have had to purchase snacks and drinks for school fundraisers not knowing how I'm going to afford them or purchase them at a reasonable price. Especially, for us to make a good profit. Snacks I would sell for fifty cents to one dollar each were purchased for thirty to fifty cents or less. Drinks sold for a dollar were purchased for five to ten cents each. Most came from an agency getting surplus items from local groceries. But, like Sam's and Costco, they might have items one

time you go there and then they disappear for a long time, or you may never see them again. Every time I have needed these items, they "miraculously" appear even though it may be months before I needed them again.

4) Hurricane Irma found its way to us a few months ago posing some challenges. Putting up hurricane shutters the day before it hit revealed missing bolts. Rushing to Lowes, I was told they had been sold out for quite some time. The sale's clerk said he would check to make sure. He came back holding one box, saying it must have been a return. I wonder how many people had been told they were sold out before I got the last box.

5) Also needing generator oil the day after the hurricane, I went to almost every place I could find open, but to no avail. Returning towards home, I saw Lowe's was now open. I'm thinking, "No place else has had it, I'm sure they're out too." I stopped anyway. Asking directions to generator oil, I found one last bottle of the weight I needed.

6) After a seemingly endless search for a Christmas tree, my wife and I finally agreed on one. Then we were told it was out of stock. I asked if we could purchase the display. After a long search for the department manager, we were told "yes". Wanting the best deal I could get; I asked if the price could be reduced. The tree price was already reduced 20%. I was a surprised when they gave an additional 15% off. I was even more surprised when I got to the register. I almost didn't show my veterans card thinking, "There's no way they'll give me an additional 10% off", but they did.

For I know the plans I have for you," says the LORD. "They are plans for good and not for disaster, to give you a future and a hope" (Jeremiah 29:11).

Time, space, and your attention would fail if I recounted all the events I can remember. My life's "deal stories" reminds me of the Bible verse speaking of all the things Jesus said and did, *"Jesus also did many other things. If they were all written down, I suppose the whole world could not contain the books that would be written"* (John 21:25). I wouldn't come close to innumerable volumes, but I could write a few.

Many times, I've prayed for a good parking space, green traffic lights, especially when I'm running late, or help finding a lost or misplaced item, and God gives it to me. Not every time, but most of the time. He often gives those things to me even when I forget to ask Him.

Thank you, Lord, for your unending blessings. You certainly are greatly concerned about the BIG little things in our lives. *"Casting all your cares [all your anxieties, all your worries, and all your concerns, once and for all] on Him, for He cares about you [with deepest affection, and watches over you very carefully]"* (1 Peter 5:7 AMP). *"Look at the ravens. They don't plant or harvest or store food in barns, for God feeds them. And you are far more valuable to him than any birds! Look at the lilies and how they grow. They don't work or make their clothing, yet Solomon in all his glory was not dressed as beautifully as they are. And if God cares so wonderfully for flowers that are here today and thrown into the fire tomorrow, he will certainly care for you. Why do you have so little faith?"* (Luke 12:24,27,28).

Chapter 35: Absolutes

We seldom use them accurately. Even if our declarations and accusations are partially or mostly true. Absolutes leave no room for exceptions.

Fill in the blanks: You never _____. I always _____. How often can we use the words all, always, every, never, nothing, none, impossible, incomparable, perfect, best, worst, or irreconcilable as true absolutes? Maybe in certain contexts they might hold some validity. Often, they are used incorrectly.

A common reason given for divorce is "irreconcilable differences." This implies, no declares, there is absolutely no way there could be reconciliation. Until every means and way to reconcile has been exhausted, can this be an accurate statement? I'm not saying there is always a way to reconcile. I've been through two unwanted divorces. It only takes one party to prevent any possibility of reversal.

The Bible is full of absolutes. Look at how many times these words are used (what version is chosen determines the exact count):

- "all" - 5,878,
- "every" - 2,112,
- "never" - 631,
- "none" - 447, and
- "perfect" - 176.

The list goes on and on.

Second Timothy 3:16 states, "*All Scripture is inspired by God and is useful to teach us what is true and to make us realize what is wrong in our lives. It corrects us when we are wrong and teaches us to do what is right*". It does not say most, or the majority, of the Bible is God's Word. Many people do not believe the Bible is entirely the Word of God. Religions often pick and choose what to believe and what not to believe. Thus, resulting in a multitude of differing theologies.

Old or New Testament, the gospel message is the same: '*But he was pierced for our rebellion, crushed for our sins. He was beaten so we could be whole. He was whipped so we could be healed. **All** of us, like sheep, have strayed away. We have left God's paths to follow our own. Yet the LORD laid on him the sins of us **all***" (Isaiah 53:5-6).

Two different writers, Isaiah, and Paul, (~800 years apart) penned God's same message: "*For **everyone** has sinned; we **all** fall short of God's glorious standard; For the wages of sin is death, but the free gift of God is **eternal** life through Christ Jesus our Lord*" (Romans 3:23, 6:23).

More absolutes: "*I give them **eternal** life, and they will **never** perish. **No one** can snatch them away from me*" (John 10:28).

One of the most well-known verses in the Bible is loaded with absolutes: "*For this is how God loved the **world**: He gave his one and **only** Son, so that **everyone** who believes in him will **not** perish, but have **eternal** life*" (John 3:16).

Absolute assurance is given to **everyone** who puts their **complete** trust in the **total** payment the Lord Jesus Christ has made **once** for **all** sin and sinners.

"*What shall we say about such wonderful things as these? If God is for us, who can ever be against us? Since he did not spare even his own Son but gave him up for us all, won't he also give us everything else? Who dares accuse us whom God has chosen for his own? No one—for God himself has given us right standing with himself. Who then will condemn us? No one—for Christ Jesus died for us and was raised to life for us, and he is sitting in the place of honor at God's right hand, pleading for us. Can anything ever separate us from Christ's love? Does it mean he no longer loves us if we have trouble or calamity, or are persecuted, or hungry, or destitute, or in danger, or threatened with death? No, despite all these things, overwhelming victory is ours through Christ, who loved us. And I am convinced that **nothing can ever separate us from God's love**. Neither death nor life, neither angels nor demons,*neither our fears for today nor our worries about tomorrow—not even the powers of hell can separate us from God's love. No power in the sky above or in the earth below—indeed, nothing in all creation will ever be able to separate us from the love of God that is revealed in Christ Jesus our Lord*" (Romans 8:31-35,37-39). Can you think of any absolute or exception left out of this passage?

Speaking of the question "Is the Lord Jesus really coming back to take His children to heaven?" 2 Peter 3:9 says, "*The Lord isn't really being slow about his promise, as some people think. No, he is being patient for your sake. He does not want anyone to be destroyed, but wants **everyone** to repent. He wants to give everyone as much time as possible to change their minds (repent) and trust Him alone as their Savior.*"

There is only one true God who came to earth as the Lord Jesus Christ and can be **absolutely** trusted. "*He showed you these things so you would know that the LORD is God and there is no other*" (Deuteronomy 4:35).

"*I have written this to you who believe in the name of the Son of God, so that you may **know** you have eternal life*" (1 John 5:13).

Are you absolutely certain you're absolutely saved? There's no better absolute!

Chapter 36: A Left Out and Distorted Bible

How many times have we misunderstood what someone is trying to convey to us? Ever play the game where everyone sits in a circle and one person whispers something to the person beside them. Each person repeats the message they heard to whomever is seated next to them. At the end, the last one tells everyone what they heard. Laughs burst out hearing the distortion.

Why do you think there are so many different religions stating they believe in God and the Bible? How can we determine who has the truth God wants us to hear and apply it to our lives?

Initially we might quote John 16:13a, *"When the Spirit of truth comes, he will guide you into all truth."* No doubt, when we ask for and rely only on the guidance and wisdom of God's Holy Spirit inside of us to reveal the truth of Scripture, He will. Are there any roadblocks?

I would list at least two:

1) Our beliefs being based on our upbringing and experiences. Specifically, what we have been taught by parents, pastors, and educational systems, including Bible colleges and seminaries.

2) As the late Dr. Cambron, (one of my Bible college professors), would say, "Read the rest of the verse, or read the surrounding verses."

You can prove anything from the Bible if you take it out of context. I remember being told the following, at a Bible college no less (I'm wanting to prove a point, not be sacrilegious):

• Did you know that baseball in in the Bible? ... In the **big-inning**

• Motorcycle is in the Bible ...The sound of David's **Triumph** was heard throughout the land.

• Tennis is in the Bible ... Joseph **served in the courts** of Pharoah.

• Cigarettes are in the Bible ... Sarah lit upon her **Camel**.

• Football is in the Bible ... "Moses was **left-back** in Egypt."

• The Bible prohibits TVs ... **Tell-a-vision** to no man. Nowadays, it's not a bad idea.

Here are some Bible verses illustrating the distortion resulting from "left outs". You've probably heard these partial quotes from Bible verses:

• *"And we know that God causes everything to work together for the good"* (Romans 8:28a).

119

• *"The earnest prayer of a righteous person has great power and produces wonderful results"* (James 5:16b NKJV)

• *"Bring all the tithes into the storehouse so there will be enough food in my Temple. 'If you do,"* says the LORD of Heaven's Armies, *'I will open the windows of heaven for you. I will pour out a blessing so great you won't have enough room to take it in! Try it! Put me to the test!'"* (Malachi 3:10).

• *"Wives, submit to your own husbands, as to the Lord. For the husband is the head of the wife even as Christ is the head of the church, his body, and is himself its Savior. Now as the church submits to Christ, so also wives should submit in everything to their husbands"* (Ephesians 5:22-24).

Now for the "left out" parts:

• Romans 8:28b - the condition for God's promise: *"for those who are called according to His purpose."* Only as we are asking for and seeking God's perfect will for our lives can we claim this promise.

• James 5:16a - A conditional command: *"Confess your sins to each other and pray for each other so that you may be healed."* Certainly, we should choose carefully whom we share our sins with. A trusted friend is essential. But don't expect maximum prayer power without obeying God's command in the first part of this verse.

• Malachi 3:10 is used to promote a prosperity message. Give to God and His ministry and He will send a deluge of blessings beyond your wildest dreams. A better version (ESV) reads: *"Bring the full tithe into the storehouse, that there may be food in my house. And thereby put me to the test, says the LORD of hosts, if I will not open the windows of heaven for you and pour down for you a blessing **until there is no more need**."*

God promises He will supply our needs, not wants or greed. *"And this same God who takes care of me will supply all your needs from his glorious riches, which have been given to us in Christ Jesus"* (Philippians 4:19).

He also promises in Psalm 84:11 *"For the LORD God is our sun and our shield. He gives us grace and glory. The LORD will withhold no good thing from those who do what is right."* What would be the corresponding promise to those not doing what is right?

Praise God He does not deal with us on a deserving basis. *"He has not dealt with us according to our sins, Nor punished us according to our iniquities"* (Psalm 103:10 NKJV).

• Before pronouncing Ephesians 5:22-24 judgment on wives, read verses 25 and 28. *"For husbands, this means love your wives, just as Christ loved the church. In the same way, husbands ought to love their wives as they love their own bodies. For a man who loves his wife actually shows love for himself."*

What wife would experience any difficulty submitting to a husband who is striving to love her like he loves himself?

This speaks to me when my wife, Joyce, wants to go to the beach and I have other plans or "more important" things to do. She loves to go to the beach. Not my first choice unless I'm fishing or collecting shells for a craft. But I have started to abandon some of my plans for hers.

"Don't be selfish; don't try to impress others. Be humble, thinking of others as better than yourselves" (Philippians 2:3).

May we strive daily to not leave anything out of God's Word and avoid distortion.

Especially by reading the context of verses and comparing hard to understand verses or passages with clear, easy to understand ones. This may mean even changing our thoughts and actions if they do not align with God's truth revealed through His Holy Spirit.

Pay attention to the warning in Revelation 22:18-19. *"And I solemnly declare to everyone who hears the words of prophecy written in this book: If anyone adds anything to what is written here, God will add to that person the plagues described in this book. And if anyone removes any of the words from this book of prophecy, God will remove that person's share in the tree of life and in the holy city that are described in this book."*

God doesn't want His truth to be left out or distorted.

Chapter 37: Declaration … The Greatest News Ever

A declaration is defined as "a positive, explicit, or formal statement; proclamation"[55] or "an announcement, often one that is written and official."[56]

Synonyms for declaration include proclamation, insistence, affirmation, assertion, protestation, avowal, and claim.

It's not just an everyday, ordinary statement made by someone. A declaration is usually something of great importance with a lasting effect.

If you're an American what might first come to mind as an extremely important and lasting declaration for our country. Without hesitation, the Declaration of Independence is my choice. Written over two hundred years ago.

Listen to its opening three sentence declaration: "We hold these truths to be self-evident, that all men are created equal, that they are endowed by their Creator with certain unalienable rights, that among these are life, liberty and the pursuit of happiness. That to secure these rights, governments are instituted among men, deriving their just powers from the consent of the governed. That whenever any form of government becomes destructive to these ends, it is the right of the people to alter or to abolish it, and to institute new government, laying its foundation on such principles and organizing its powers in such form, as to them shall seem most likely to effect their safety and happiness."

The Bible is overflowing with declarations. *"Who declared it from the beginning, that we might know, and beforehand, that we might say, 'He is right?' There was none who declared it, none who proclaimed, none who heard your words"* (Isaiah 41:26a ESV).

This may sound like a question being asked as if *who knows the answer?* Here's the answer: *"For behold, He who forms mountains, And creates the wind, Who **declares** to man what his thought is, And makes the morning darkness, Who treads the high places of the earth— The Lord God of hosts is His name"* (Amos 4:13 NKJV).

---

[55] (https://www.dictionary.com/browse/declaration),
[56] (https://dictionary.cambridge.org/us/dictionary/english/declaration)

The Bible tells us to declare the greatest gospel message ever. *"And he said to them, 'Go into all the world and proclaim the gospel to the whole creation'"* (Mark 16:15 ESV).

We are also to declare God's righteousness to everyone everywhere. We declare God's righteousness by the way we live our lives. *"And now, dear brothers and sisters, one final thing. Fix your thoughts on what is true, and honorable, and right, and pure, and lovely, and admirable. Think about things that are excellent and worthy of praise"* (Philippians 4:8).

"The people whom I formed for myself, that they might declare my praise" (Isaiah 43:21 ESV)

It doesn't stop with us. Scripture tells us all of God's creation declares His glory.

"The heavens proclaim the glory of God. The skies display his craftsmanship" (Psalm 19:1).

"Praise the LORD! Praise the LORD from the heavens! Praise him from the skies! Praise him, all his angels! Praise him, all the armies of heaven! Praise him, sun and moon! Praise him, all you twinkling stars! Praise him, skies above! Praise him, vapors high above the clouds! Let every created thing give praise to the LORD, for he issued his command, and they came into being. He set them in place forever and ever. His decree will never be revoked. Praise the LORD from the earth, you creatures of the ocean depths, fire and hail, snow and clouds, wind and weather that obey him, mountains and all hills, fruit trees and all cedars, wild animals and all livestock, small scurrying animals and birds," (Psalm 148:1-10). I don't think God left anything out.

God's Word continues: *"Just ask the animals, and they will teach you. Ask the birds of the sky, and they will tell you. Speak to the earth, and it will instruct you. Let the fish in the sea speak to you. For they all know that my disaster has come from the hand of the LORD. For the life of every living thing is in his hand, and the breath of every human being"* (Job 12:7-10).

"Let the heavens be glad, and the earth rejoice! Let the sea and everything in it shout his praise! Let the fields and their crops burst out with joy! Let the trees of the forest sing for joy before the LORD, for he is coming!" (Psalm 96:11-13) *"You will live in joy and peace. The mountains and hills will burst into song, and the trees of the field will clap their hands!"* (Isaiah 55:12).

The greatest declarations of all time are as follows:

All human beings are condemned:

"All of us, like sheep, have strayed away. We have left God's paths to follow our own" (Isaiah 53:6a). *"For everyone has sinned; we all fall short of God's glorious standard"* (Romans 3:23).

God's standard for eternal life in heaven is absolute perfection. Not even one lie can enter.

*"But there shall by **no means** enter it anything that defiles, or causes an abomination or **a lie**, but only those who are written in the Lamb's Book of Life"* (Revelation 21:27a NKJV).

By accepting Christ's payment for all our sins, we receive His perfection:

"For God made Christ, who never sinned, to be the offering for our sin, so that we could be made right with God through Christ" (2 Corinthians 5:21). *"For He made Him who knew no sin to be sin for us, that we might become the righteousness of God in Him"* (NKJV).

All sin for everyone is completely paid for. Unacceptance is the only reason anyone will be separated from God forever.

"Yet the LORD laid on him the sins of us all" (Isaiah 53:6b) *"He himself is the sacrifice that atones for our sins—and not only our sins but the sins of all the world"* (1 John:2:2).

Eternal life in heaven is a free gift given to everyone who places their complete faith and trust in Jesus Christ:

"God saved you by his grace when you believed. And you can't take credit for this; it is a gift from God. Salvation is not a reward for the good things we have done, so none of us can boast about it" (Ephesians 2:8-9). *"For this is how God loved the world: He gave his one and only Son, so that everyone who believes in him will not perish but have eternal life. God sent his Son into the world not to judge the world, but to save the world through him. There is no judgement against anyone who believes in him. But anyone who does not believe in him has already been judged for not believing in God's one and only Son"* (*John 3:16-18*).

This gospel message is called the "Good News". I think a declaration like this should be termed "THE GREATEST NEWS," even better "THE GREATEST NEWS EVER!"

Chapter 38: Light in the Darkness

Ever been spelunking? Each year I would take my science classes into the dark shadows of a damp Missouri cave. Everyone wanted a working flashlight. But invariably, when deep into the cave, someone would want everyone to turn off their flashlights and experience utter darkness. It was so dark; you could not see your hand right in front of your face. What a difference when the first light was lit. The pitch-black darkness fled.

Lots of kids are afraid of the dark, even some of us older "kids." Home alone at night can be frightening. Without a nightlight, the boogeyman lurks under our bed. As an older kid, I remember occasional nights in the country by myself, with the closest neighbor well beyond screaming distance. Strange sounds would command my hairs to stand at attention.

Many times, I have been at Christmas services where the lights were all turned out and candles were lit from one person to another. The darkness evaporated with the first flame. Brighter and brighter illumination appeared as the multitude glowed.

In an attempt to experience what blind friends live with, I have closed my eyes and maneuvered inside my home. Even with an awareness of where things were, I would bump into them, stub a toe, and get disoriented. Finally, not taking another step. Can you imagine a lifetime in darkness?

Likewise, ungodly "eyes" bring spiritual darkness. You've probably heard "Our eyes are the gateway to our soul." "*But when your eye is unhealthy, your whole body is filled with darkness. And if the light you think you have is actually darkness, how deep that darkness is!*" (Matthew 6:23).

There's a dark message no one likes to hear, even in churches. It's about hell. Of course, I've heard a few good ole' boys let out some chuckles while proclaiming they will have a great time partying with their buddies in hell. The reality is: a tortuous hell awaits those who do not accept Christ as their Savior. Mark 9:48 shows, "*where the maggots never die and the fire never goes out.*) Other versions say "worms" instead of maggots. Maggots seem more gross to me than worms.

I've seen worms die after being flooded out of their homes, but to never die in an "unquenchable fire," an unimaginable torment beyond scary!

Speaking of unbelievers, God's Word further states, *"They are like wild waves of the sea, churning up the foam of their shameful deeds. They are like wandering stars, doomed forever to blackest darkness"* (Jude 13). Can you imagine being stuck deep in an eternal cave without any light? And hearing others screaming "Help! Let me out!" along with you?

This is the verdict: *"And the judgment is based on this fact. God's light came into the world, but people loved the darkness more than the light, for their actions were evil. All who do evil hate the light and refuse to go near it for fear their sins will be exposed"* (John 3:19-20). Note this comes immediately after John 3:16-18.

Speaking of darkness, *The Chicago Tribune* reported "Police statistics show most murders in the city happen from midnight to 4 a.m."[57] Evil abounds under the cloak of darkness.

If anyone knew of dark times, Job sure did. His ten sons and daughters died, along with all his servants, and over 10,000 animals. His wife told him to curse God and die. His friends brought all kinds of accusations against him. And if that weren't enough, he was covered from head to toe with boils. Yet, after all this, Job said: *"I came naked from my mother's womb, and I will be naked when I leave. The Lord gave me what I had, and the Lord has taken it away. Praise the name of the Lord!"* (Job 1:21).

In Job 12:22, he declares, *"He uncovers mysteries hidden in darkness; he brings light to the deepest gloom."* As if in summary, Job 1:22 records, (*In all of this, Job did not sin by blaming God*). Oh, to see the Light as Job did!

There's a bright light in all this darkness. The Bible is full of light. As children of God, we are given a brilliant directing source of light. *"Your word is a lamp to guide my feet and a light for my path"* (Psalm 119:105).

Jesus laid claim to being the brightest light on earth in John 8:12. *"I am the light of the world. If you follow me, you won't have to walk in darkness, because you will have the light that leads to life."*

John 1:4-5 announces, *"The Word gave life to everything that was created, and his life brought light to everyone. The light shines in the darkness, and the darkness can never extinguish it."*

It's hard to imagine a place with no darkness. Hallelujah! Heaven will be a place filled with light. *"There will be no more night. And there will be no night there—no need for lamps or sun—for the Lord God will shine on them. And they will reign forever and ever"* (Revelation 22:5).

Christians are called to be light to a darkened world. *"You are the light of the world—like a city on a hilltop that cannot be hidden. No one lights a lamp and then puts it under a basket. Instead, a lamp is placed on a stand, where it gives light to everyone in the house"* (Matthew 5:14-15).

As a child in church, I sang "This Little Light of Mine." The words still flood my mind. Each verse ended with: "I'm going to let it shine, let it shine, let it shine, let it shine."

Hand motions for the song amplified its meaning:

---

[57] (https://www.chicagotribune.com/news/ct-xpm-2009-10-20-0910200159-story.html)

• First, a finger held up as a light, moving all around my neighborhood.
• Next, one hand cupped over the finger as a bushel, and quickly removing it shouting:
   "No, I'm gonna let it shine!"
• Then, declaring with a quick blast, even Satan was not going to blow it out.
• Finally, pointing toward heaven promising I would let it shine 'til Jesus comes.

A lasting memory of what our lives should be like awaiting heaven.

The good news, the greatest news ever: Jesus suffered death and dark separation from the Father on a cross, paying for the sins of all mankind. *"He himself is the sacrifice that atones for our sins—and not only our sins but the sins of all the world"* (1 John 2:2). By placing your trust in the Lord Jesus Christ alone and accepting His complete payment for all your sin, you are assured of an eternal home in heaven. *"I tell you the truth, anyone who believes has eternal life"* (John 6:47). There is no longer fear of eternal darkness separated from God. *"For once you were full of darkness, but now you have light from the Lord. So live as people of light!"* (Ephesians 5:8)

Afraid of the deep cave of eternal darkness? I'm not, and you don't have to be either. Let the Son shine in!

Chapter 39: Go to Hell

Ever been mad enough to say this to someone or wish they were there? If you know the Bible's description of the place of eternal punishment, it might create a stop sign in your mind.

Listen to how the Bible describes hell and those who live there: *"where the maggots never die and the fire never goes out"* (Mark 9:48); *"raging waves of the sea, foaming up their own shame; wandering stars for whom is reserved the blackness of darkness forever"* (Jude 13).

Many religions do not believe in a literal hell, a place of eternal punishment.

Have you ever heard someone say, "Go to heaven." Some people and religions don't believe in a literal heaven or hell. Maybe you just die and cease to exist. If so, "live it up while you can" would be the mantra.

A more reasonable and attractive belief is: "Everyone's going to heaven, just going their own way." This persuasive argument is based on the rationalization: "How could a God who loves everyone (John 3:16) send anyone to hell?" The two verses following this well-known verse explain how He could: *"For God did not send his Son into the world to condemn the world, but in order that the world might be saved through him. Whoever believes in him is not condemned, but whoever does not believe is condemned already, because he has not believed in the name of the only Son of God."* Yes, God loves everyone and wants everyone to go to heaven, but the choice of belief or unbelief is left to them.

The consequence for unbelief is condemnation. What must one believe to not be condemned?

First: *For everyone has sinned; we all fall short of God's glorious standard"* (Romans 3:2). No matter how "good" someone is, no one is perfect. Heaven is a perfect place. To get there you must be perfect. *"But there shall by no means enter it anything that defiles, or causes an abomination or a lie, but only those who are written in the Lamb's Book of Life"* (Revelation 21:27 NKJV). Has anyone never told a lie? So, how can anyone meet the perfection requirement for heaven.

Answer: *"For He* (God) *made Him* (Christ) *who knew no sin to be sin for us, that we might become the righteousness of God in Him"* (2 Corinthians 5:21 NKJV). *"He himself is the sacrifice that atones for our sins—and not only our sins but the sins of all the world"* (1 John 2:2 NIV) Not only the sins of all born-again believers are paid for, but also every sin of all unbelievers. *"Amazing Grace"* and *"Grace Greater Than All Our Sin"* (hymns declaring the same message as 1 John 2:2).

Last and most importantly: *"God saved you by his grace when you believed. And you can't take credit for this; it is a gift from God. Salvation is not a reward for the good things we have done, so none of us can boast about it"* (Ephesians 2:8-9).

Grace is getting what we don't deserve. No amount of good works can merit eternal life in a perfect heaven. It would no longer be a gift of grace if there were other requirements in addition to belief. *"And if by grace, then it is no longer of works; otherwise grace is no longer grace. But if it is of works, it is no longer grace; otherwise work is no longer work"* (Romans 11:6 NKJV). It's one or the other. It can't be both, part one and part the other. A lot of religions will tell you it's both. They say you must trust Christ as your Savior, but then give a list of things you must do or stop doing in order to be saved or not lose your salvation.

Only by placing our trust in the complete payment the Lord Jesus Christ has paid for all our sin can we be assured of eternal life in heaven. *"I give them eternal life, and they will never perish No one can snatch them away from me"* (John 10:28). If you can lose your salvation, then it's not eternal. It's not salvation.

No one will ever go to hell because they are a sinner. All sin is paid for. The only reason anyone will spend an eternity in hell, separated from God, is their neglect or refusal to accept and place their trust in the payment for all their sin.

Place your trust in Christ alone. Then if someone tells you to "Go to hell," you can tell them why you're not going there, and they don't have to either.

Chapter 40: Easy "Believism"

I've heard it said telling someone all they have to do to go to heaven is just believe and trust Christ as your Savior is "easy believism."

Is it easy to believe and trust this message: The Lord Jesus Christ died on a cross and paid for the entire sins of every single person who will ever live? For some people it may be easy, but for others it may be very difficult.

When one considers the many different beliefs concerning questions like these: "Is there life after death?", "How can anyone know which belief is true?", "How could a God of love send anyone to hell?" It doesn't seem easy to know what to believe.

But when you see the many facts proving the Bible had to be God's Word, not man's and understand a simple gospel message of salvation, it can be easy to place your trust in the Lord Jesus Christ as your one and only Savior.

At the same time, it defies man's logic. Come on, the only way anyone can get to a perfect heaven is by simply believing, and it's free. Nothing's free. Read the fine print.

If you're old enough, you may remember when a lot of gas stations had big signs saying "Free Car Wash." Then down in real small print at the bottom it would say "with fill-up" or a minimum number of gallons purchased. See, nothing's free.

This is why so many religions will somehow include some type of human effort as a part of meriting eternal life in heaven. It only makes sense.

A serious caution must be made. In no way does the Bible say just trust Christ alone and his complete payment for all your sins, and it doesn't matter how you live your life. The rest of the Bible written in addition to the only true way to have eternal life, tells us how God wants us to live our lives as His children. Not to become His children or remain His children, but because we are His children, and He wants the very best for us.

We are born into our earthly families. We didn't have a choice, although some wish they did. Any parent who loves their children will not disown them or kick them out of their home because they disobey them. The same is true of our Heavenly Father. *"I give them eternal life, and they will never perish. No one can snatch them away from me,"* (John 10:28).

But, just as any good, loving parent will do, there will be a punishment or consequence for disobedience. God's Word puts it harshly: *"If God doesn't discipline you as he does all of his children, it means that you are illegitimate and are not really his children at all"* (Hebrews 12:8).

Different children with different personalities require different forms of punishment or consequence for their disobedience, to get favorable results ... favorable for the parents, not necessarily the children. Likewise, God disciplines His children in different ways. Look at the examples throughout the Bible. David lost his son because of his sin. Moses couldn't enter the Promised Land due to his disobedience. The prophet Zechariah lost his voice and hearing until his child was born because of his unbelief. The Israelites were repeatedly led into captivity as a result of their sin. The list goes on and on.

My two sons are also good examples of this. The best means of discipline for the oldest child was spanking. We were amazed to receive a call from school soon after the youngest started school. We were told he laughed when they spanked him for misbehaving. Yet if you looked harshly at him, it usually worked. Both eventually responded correctly to privileges being taken away for disobedience.

I remember a comedian on a cruise we took talking about how he was disciplined physically when he was young. He said today it's very difficult to use corporal punishment, especially in public. Having gone on many cruises, he tells of a time when he saw a woman who was extremely frustrated because she could not physically discipline her son onboard the cruise line. He went up to her and pointed to a corner where no one was and told her to take him over there and he would stand guard.

Parents and teachers being unable to use corporal punishment on kids now-a-days is unfortunate. Granted some parents misuse and abuse physical punishment. Scripture says very pointedly, *"Those who love their children care enough to discipline them"* (Proverbs 13:24). Even though the phrase "Spare the rod, spoil the child" is not found in the Bible, its principle is. *"Those who spare the rod of discipline hate their children. Those who love their children care enough to discipline them"* (Proverbs 13:24).

We must be careful of assuming major problems or difficulties in a person's life is automatically a result of some kind of sin. An example from the Bible is found in John 9:1-2, *"As Jesus was walking along, he saw a man who had been blind from birth. 'Rabbi,' his disciples asked him, 'why was this man born blind? Was it because of his own sins or his parents' sins?'"* They did not just ask Jesus why the man was born blind, but automatically assumed it was because of someone's sin. *"Jesus answered them, 'It was not because of his sins or his parent's sins. This happened so the power of God could be seen in him.'"*

Why do bad things happen to good people?

How can a loving God allow bad things to happen to good/righteous people? Wouldn't a just and loving God reserve bad things for bad people and leave the good for the good ones?

Job is probably the best example of more bad things happening to the most righteous man alive in his world.

Just to lose seven sons and three daughters in one day with a freak accident would bring a "why me" question. Shortly thereafter he receives word that his servants have been killed and all his 10,000 livestock have been stolen. And if that weren't enough, he was covered from head-to-toe with boils.

I would certainly look to my wife for comfort after all this. Not Job's, she told him to curse God and die.

Without a doubt, the only earthly resources he had left was his closest friends. But his friends gave no encouragement. They brought all kinds of accusations against him.

What's utterly amazing is the record in Job 1:21-22: *"Yet, after all this, Job said: The Lord gave & the Lord has taken away; may the name of the Lord be praised. In all this, Job did not sin by charging God with wrongdoing."* Would you or I respond like Job if those things happened to us?

There are three reasons given in God's Word for Him bringing or allowing bad things to happen to His children:

1. **To increase our faith and trust in God**.
   "We can rejoice, too, when we run into problems and trials, for we know that they help us develop endurance. And endurance develops strength of character, and character strengthens our confident hope of salvation. [5] And this hope will not lead to disappointment. For we know how dearly God loves us, because he has given us the Holy Spirit to fill our hearts with his love" (Romans 5:3-5).

   "Dear brothers and sisters, when troubles of any kind come your way, consider it an opportunity for great joy. For you know that when your faith is tested, your endurance has a chance to grow" (James 1:2-3).

There are two possible responses to bad things: You either get bitter, or you get better. It's easy to get bitter. Not so much to get better.

2. **So we can be a great testimony to others**. *In the same way, let your good deeds shine out for all to see, so that everyone will praise your heavenly Father"* (Matthew 5:16).

Job's testimony certainly was powerful to his condemning wife, friends, and many others, including us today. I'm sure the news tablets had a front "page" article on Job.

3. **So we can relate to and understand the same or similar things others are going through** and encourage them. **"**So encourage each other and build each other up, just as you are already doing"* (1 Thessalonians 5:11).

Ever have someone say they know what you are going through, even though they've never gone through anything like you have? Don't you think, "Yeah, right?"

Why does God not heal all His children who suffer through terrible health issues. Paul who wrote more books of the Bible than anyone else (13 or 14 books), certainly had enough faith or trust in the Lord to heal him of a serious "thorn in the flesh." Three times he pleaded with the Lord to heal him. He finally realized: *"Even though I have received such wonderful revelations from God. So to keep me from becoming proud, I was given a thorn in my flesh, a messenger from Satan to torment me and keep me from becoming proud. Three different times I begged the Lord to take it away. Each time he said, 'My grace is all you need. My power works best in weakness.' So now I am glad to boast about my weaknesses, so that the power of Christ can work through me. That's why I take pleasure in my weaknesses, and in the insults, hardships, persecutions, and troubles that I suffer for Christ. For when I am weak, then I am strong"* (2 Corinthians 12:7-10).

If nothing "bad" ever happened to us. would we need God, His Word, the Bible, or the power of His Holy Spirit as much? The word "bad" was put in parenthesis because I believe in God's vocabulary or plans there no such thing, except His hatred of sin. *"For I know the plans I have for you,' says the LORD. "They are plans for good and not for disaster, to give you a future and a hope"* (Jeremiah 29:11). *"And we know that God causes everything to work together for the good of those who love God and are called according to his purpose for them"* (Romans 8:28). Don't leave off the condition on the last half of this verse.

"How else can we obey God's commandment to rejoice in all things? Always be joyful. Be thankful in all circumstances, for this is God's will for you who belong to Christ Jesus" (1 Thessalonians 5:16,18).

Back to "easy 'believism.'" God has done the hard part. Harder than anyone else has ever done. *"But God showed his great love for us by sending Christ to die for us while we were still sinners"* (Romans 5:8). We're left with the easy part. Like the well-known song says, "Amazing grace how sweet the sound, that saved a wretch like me." But don't leave out the hard part as His born-again child. Obey God and His Word. Not for salvation or to keep it, but a heart response of love for what He's done for you and me.

Chapter 41: "Christanese"

There are many commonly used words and phrases that do NOT clearly communicate the one & only true gospel message, the greatest message on earth. They can be very perplexing, even deceptive.

Here's some of the confusing words and phrases:

1. **"born-again"** – What was Nicodemus' response when Jesus told him no one could go to heaven without being "born again?"

"Jesus replied, 'Very truly I tell you, no one can see the kingdom of God unless they are born again.' How can someone be born when they are old?' Nicodemus asked. Surely they cannot enter a second time into their mother's womb to be born!'" (John 3:3-4).

2. **"accept Jesus into your heart"** *"For it is with your heart that you believe and are justified..."* (Romans 10:10a). No one puts Jesus in their literal heart. Like Nicodemus, we would say it's an impossibility. What it means is don't just have an intellectual belief in Jesus Christ, but believe with your inner being, your soul, your mind. The heart of a person is not simply a mechanical pump but the center of all thought and emotion. Isn't that what we mean when we say things like "I love you with all my heart."

3. **"give your life to Jesus"** or **"make Jesus Lord of your life"** "Lord" means "master, controller." Is Jesus Lord? Most assuredly, He is the creator of everything and in total control of all things He has made.

Is Jesus Lord of everything in your life? He's not in mine. I am striving with the help of God's Word and His Holy Spirit inside of me to be more and more like the Lord Jesus Christ each day. But I know from experience and what the Bible says I am not perfect and never will be until Jesus takes me to my heavenly home. Does Jesus control everything in any believer's life? We choose to obey or disobey Him.

4. **"repent and turn from your sin"** Does a person have to repent to be saved? Yes, the Bible clearly says everyone must repent to be saved. *"Peter replied, 'Repent and be baptized, every one*

of you, in the name of Jesus Christ for the forgiveness of your sins. And you will receive the gift of the Holy Spirit'" (Acts 2:38 ESV).

Does a person have to stop doing certain sins to be saved? No, *"For it is by grace you have been saved, through faith - and this is not from yourselves, it is the gift of God—not by works, so that no one can boast"* (Ephesians 2:8-9 NIV).

The Greek word for "repent" is "metanoia" meaning "to have second thoughts, reconsider; change your mind." *"And if by grace, then it is no longer of works; otherwise grace is no longer grace. But if it is of works, it is no longer grace; otherwise work is no longer work"* (Romans 11:6 NKJV). It's one or the other, it cannot be both, or part one and part the other. We must change our minds from believing some kind of work on our part will get us to heaven. Reread the two previous verses.

"If you openly declare that Jesus is Lord and believe in your heart that God raised him from the dead, you will be saved" (Romans 10:9).

Make the gospel message crystal clear. It's the greatest news ever proclaimed.

Chapter 42: My Testimony

My father was a pastor ever since I was five years old. I was in church almost every time the door was opened. As I grew up, I was very active in church. I was president of the youth group, played on church softball, basketball, and bowling teams. I sang solos in church and was in the church choir. My dad even had me give messages sometimes.

I heard the gospel clearly presented time and time again. But I still thought the first ones God would allow into heaven would certainly be preachers. Next in line would be their family members.

Now if you've had much experience with PK's (Preacher's Kids), you will find a lot of them being pretty mischievous. Often, they live very ungodly lives when they get out on their own. Such was the case of my younger brother who stopped going to church and hung out with the wrong crowd. But I was not like my brother or some PKs.

What it boiled down to was my thinking I was good enough to get to heaven on my own and certainly with my father's calling and reputation.

It wasn't until I was twelve years old, I changed my way of thinking. An evangelist friend of my father was holding a series of revival meetings at our church. Once again, hearing a clear gospel message, I finally realized I was not good enough to get to heaven on my dad's merits, nor my own.

During those meetings I placed my complete trust in the payment Jesus Christ had made on the cross for all my sins.

Unfortunately, there are many people, who like me, think either they or a family member are good enough to have their entry ticket for heaven stamped by God. It doesn't matter how good or how bad you are, whether you or your family live exemplary lives or ungodly lives, nothing anyone can do is good enough to get them into a perfect heaven. Likewise, there's nothing anyone has done bad enough to keep them out of heaven. There's only one free way to heaven. It's by accepting the complete payment a perfect Jesus made for all your sins.

This is not my idea, it's God's. There are a multitude of different ideas on how a person gets to heaven. But Jesus himself said he was the one and only way to heaven.

My plea to you is to base what you believe on clear easy to understand verses from the Bible. Look at the verses repeated over and over in this book being quoted from the Bible.

Place your complete trust in God's Word, the Bible, which is full of fact after fact proving it to be totally the Word of God, not man.

About the Author

Author Larry Hoffeditz has degrees in Natural Science, Behavioral Science, and Biblical Education. He taught science courses in urban, rural, private, and inner-city high schools for 25 years. The courses taught include Chemistry, Biology, Marine Science, Physical Science, Earth Science, Environmental Science, Material Science and Technology, and Physics. He also was a professor at Florida Bible College. Teaching Bible studies at his church, and *The Source* homeless ministry are part of his weekly schedule.

He has worked in a wide variety of medical facilities including, hospitals, nursing homes, pharmacies, and nuclear pharmaceutical and chemical facilities.

He is a published author in Focus on the Family publications and EA Publisher's *Anchor in the Storm,* Volumes 1 and 2.

Larry is on staff at the annual Florida Christian Writers Conference where he has attended for many years. He also assists at The Well Christian Writers Conference in Grand Rapids, MI, and is a Word Weavers critique group member.

He is a driver and employment specialist for RISE, an organization that provides daily training programs and activities for disabled clients.

Larry and his beautiful Filipino wife, Joyce, reside in Vero Beach, FL. They are actively involved in their church ministries. They facilitate a Joy Group and volunteer for MFI (Missionary Flights), CareNet crisis pregnancy, Safe Families, The Source, and Florida Disaster Relief.

They love to fish and crab, kayak, go thrifting, and do gardening. They sell their crafts at local shows. Both were former high school science teachers for more than 20 years.

Five grandkids, two sons and their wives, and Sheba, their Alaskan Malamute dog, complete this blessed family. Pictures are available on request.

Made in the USA
Columbia, SC
03 September 2023

22380107R00078